CHRIS SIDWELLS

KT-561-031

Really Wild Cycling

THE **POCKET GUIDE** TO
OFF-THE-BEATEN-TRACK
CHALLENGES

ROBINSON

ROBINSON

First published in Great Britain
in 2020 by Robinson

10 9 8 7 6 5 4 3 2 1

Copyright © Chris Sidwells, 2020

Photographs on pages 13, 17, 19, 68, 69, 74, 75, 76,
79, 82, 83, 85, 87, 117, 118, 119, 125, 126, 153, 156, 157,
158, 159, 166, 167, 173, 175, 177, 180, 181, 183, 185, 188,
189, 190, 191, 193, 196, 197, 216, 217, 219, 220, 221, 222,
225, 228 and 243 copyright © Andy Jones
Photographs on pages 6, 7, 20, 21, 45, 49, 51, 53,
56, 57, 58, 59, 61, 62, 67, 129, 132, 133, 135 and 137
copyright © Jess Anez and Ed Jackson
Photographs on pages 5, 103, 108 and 109
copyright © Paul Gregory
Photographs on pages 95, 99, 100 and 101
copyright © William Alves and Carol Parsons
Photographs on pages 35, 235 and 241
copyright © Simone Warner
Photograph on page 23 copyright
© Luke Edwardes-Evans
All other photographs © Chris Sidwells

The moral right of the author has been asserted.

A CIP catalogue record for this book
is available from the British Library.

ISBN 978-1-47214-372-3

Typeset in Neutra and Sentinel
Designed by Andrew Barron @ thextension
Maps and diagrams by Cedric Knight
Printed and bound in China by
C&C Offset Printing Co., Ltd.

Papers used by Robinson are from
well-managed forests and other
responsible sources.

MIX
Paper from
responsible sources
FSC® C104740
www.fsc.org

Robinson
An imprint of
Little, Brown Book Group
Carmelite House
50 Victoria Embankment
London EC4Y 0DZ

An Hachette UK Company
www.hachette.co.uk

www.littlebrown.co.uk

To all cyclists who love to get out the maps
and go where they have never ridden, don't ever lose
your wonder about what is down that road, behind
that hill or beyond that horizon.

CONTENTS

CHAPTER 1   **REALLY WILD CYCLING**
What this book is about and some things
to consider   2

RIDE 1   AROUND YOUR TOWN   12

CHAPTER 2   **SOUTH AND SOUTH-WEST OF ENGLAND**   20

RIDE 2   THE DOWNS LINK   22

RIDE 3   THE SOUTH DOWNS TRAVERSE   30

RIDE 4   THE RIDGEWAY   36

RIDE 5   THE TOUR DE TORS   44

RIDE 6   DEVON COASTAL HILL-FEST   52

RIDE 7   CORNISH COAST-TO-COAST (AND BACK)   60

CHAPTER 3   **CENTRAL ENGLAND**   68

RIDE 8   CROSSING THE COTSWOLDS   70

RIDE 9   ICKLE BIT OF ICKNIELD   80

RIDE 10   CRISS-CROSSING THE LONG MYND   88

RIDE 11   RAGGED STAFF   94

RIDE 12   HARDCORE 100   102

RIDE 13   SPINAL TAP   110

CHAPTER 4   **WALES**   118

RIDE 14   SAMPLING SARN HELEN   120

RIDE 15   ON THE BEACHES   128

RIDE 16   HEAVEN AND HELL   138

RIDE 17   WILD ROAD TO WORLD'S END   144

CHAPTER 5   **NORTHERN ENGLAND**   150

RIDE 18   TRANS-PENNINE TRAIL CENTRAL   152

RIDE 19   THE MARY TOWNELEY LOOP   160

RIDE 20   THE PENNINE BRIDLEWAY   168

RIDE 21   WOLDS WAY BY BIKE   176

RIDE 22   THE THREE PEAKS CYCLO-CROSS   184

RIDE 23   SALTER FELL BOTH WAYS   192

RIDE 24   COAST-TO-COAST, PART ONE   200

RIDE 25   COAST-TO-COAST, PART TWO   208

RIDE 26   BACK O' SKIDDA'   216

RIDE 27   FROM SEA TO SOURCE   224

CHAPTER 6   **SCOTLAND**   232

RIDE 28   LOCH-BAGGING IN SCOTLAND   234

RIDE 29   MEALL CALA MOUNTAIN CIRCUIT   242

1

Really Wild Cycling

WHAT THIS BOOK IS ABOUT AND SOME THINGS TO CONSIDER

This book follows on from *Wild Cycling*, a pocket guide to fifty great rides off the beaten track in Britain. It adds an element of challenge to the joys of finding, planning and following routes that are quirky, adventurous or simply away from the mainstream.

As with the rides described in *Wild Cycling*, those in *Really Wild Cycling* are not necessarily prescriptive; they are not a list to be ticked off, but suggestions. They are meant to show the wild cycling potential of different parts of the country, as well as acting as templates for wild cycling challenges you put together yourself.

Just take two examples. Ride 15, On the Beaches, could be copied in any coastal area. As can ride 13, Spinal Tap, in any upland region. There are many more rides like them, challenges that can be repeated in similar areas throughout the UK and the wider world.

The other attraction of this kind of wild cycling is planning the rides. I find planning new routes as much fun as riding them, and I know I'm not alone. We are very lucky, too, with so much computer software and so many apps these days designed to help us navigate around the planet on our bikes.

My favourite maps, and the ones that I think best suit the needs of adventurous cyclists, are the Ordnance Survey (OS) 1: 50,000 scale Landranger series, which is available on memory-map GPS navigation software www. memory-map.co.uk. Using Memory Map software you can have the whole OS 1: 50,000 scale Landranger Map series on your PC, lap-top or other device. You can then upload any routes you plan to GPS navigation devices.

There are other very good maps and systems you can use, but I realise my preference for OS maps is because when I started going out and exploring on two wheels they were by far the best. I was a teenager then, and even I have to admit that was some time ago. I still enjoy it as much as ever, though. I know there is other mapping software out there, and I've heard good things about lots of it, so go with what you think is best to plan your routes and find your way.

You might already plan your own routes and bike adventures. If not, I really hope you start doing so. There's a joy to be had from looking at a map and seeing a way to cross it by cycling off-road trails and back-country lanes.

Then there's the satisfaction of having ridden the route you planned, and the bonus of setting yourself a challenge, as I've done with the rides in *Really Wild Cycling*.

Before you plan your routes, though, there are some things you need to know about access rights. The main off-road rights of way for cyclists in England and Wales are along bridleways, which are represented on the OS 1: 50,000 Landranger by long-dashed red lines. Short-dashed red lines are footpaths, and at the moment, in England at least, cyclists aren't allowed to ride along footpaths. However, there are moves to open up some footpaths to cyclists, and you can often shadow big long-distance-footpath walks. In fact, I set that as one of the challenges in this book with Ride 21, Wolds Way by Bike. Cyclist access in Scotland is different and a little less restrictive, so long as you follow the guidelines you will find on www.outdooraccess-scotland.scot.

Many of the rides in *Really Wild Cycling* use bridleways, but I have also used tiny lanes (shown in yellow on Landranger maps, the width of the yellow strip being broadly proportional to the width of the lane), as well as designated cycle routes created by bodies such as the creator of the National Cycle Network, Sustrans. I have used some designated cycle routes for part of or the whole way because they are really enjoyable to ride, and in the case of rides like 24 and 25, parts 1 and 2 of the Coast-to-Coast Route, they are challenges worth completing simply to say you have done them as well as for the sheer enjoyment they offer. Some of the rides in *Really Wild Cycling* are all on roads, but such roads are those only locals know, and even they use them infrequently.

There are other small lanes, depicted on Landranger by parallel narrow black lines. However, those lanes sometimes have local rights in force, and occasionally they are the private drive to a house or farm. The ones I use in *Really Wild Cycling* are those where I'm sure there is a right of way for cyclists. Where you have to use a surfaced lane it's better to stick to the yellow ones on the map, or those that are part of a designated cycle route.

I have used a few B-roads where it's unavoidable, and very occasionally a short stretch of A-road, although I tried to do so only if there was a cycle path running alongside it. Sometimes when you're planning a different type of challenge, as I did with Ride 1, Around Your Town, the first ride in *Really Wild Cycling* and a one-off, you have to compromise.

Around Your Town reflects the book's spirit. It's a ride right around my nearest town, Doncaster, and I did it by staying as close to the town as possible without entering it, while at the same time using bridleways, trails and back roads. I'm not expecting many people

to do this one; instead I hope you use it as a template for a ride around the margins of your nearest town. It's a fun thing both to plan and to ride.

Finally, before moving on from planning and finding your way, there is one more big thing to mention. GPS devices are a great help, but you should not rely on them. You should still take a paper map with you, and a compass, especially when going high or far. Satellite coverage cannot be guaranteed everywhere, especially in remote places. Paper maps and a standard compass will never let you down. You can print the maps from your screen if you don't want the bother of unfolding and folding a standard map. Always use a plastic map sleeve to put your map or maps in. They are cheap and available in most outdoor shops

With a map and a compass you always know where you are. OS maps are orientated roughly north to south. So lay the map out, place the compass on top of it and align the vertical grid lines with the direction of the compass needle, with the top of the map representing north. Face that direction. The map is then roughly oriented, and you should be able to relate the features illustrated on it to the features you can see around you. It's not an exact method, but it's a helpful start.

It's worth getting to know much more about maps so you are highly skilled at using them. There's a lot about map reading online; the website www.maptools.com is excellent. You could also enrol on a good map-reading course – it's really worth

signing up to one if you are unsure how to get the most out of OS maps.

A map and compass fit easily into standard cycling jerseys, and it's important to wear specific cycling kit, not just normal outdoor clothes, and dress according to the weather. Check two weather forecasts before long wild rides, and if you are going high always carry a cycling-specific rucksack. It doesn't need to be a big rucksack, but it should contain a full set of water and windproof clothing, and extra gloves in case the weather turns really bad. You can't be too cautious when taking on a bit of wild cycling. In the one competitive event I've included in *Really Wild Cycling*, the Three Peaks Cyclo-cross, the organisers insist competitors carry a survival blanket and a whistle. Both will help them stay alive if they fall or get lost.

High wild places are a joy to experience, but the potential danger is real. Even on bright, warm, sunny days in summer the weather can change quickly in high places. If you are above 300 metres or 1,000 feet in Britain it can suddenly get cold, even in summer, especially if it rains. Extra clothing and extra food are both essential. Take a first aid kit and whistle to attract attention if you have an accident. It's safer to do high, lonely rides in company with others, especially if you are inexperienced in such an environment.

A well-maintained bike is another essential. As I said in *Wild Cycling*,

I like using my cyclo-cross bike on these rides. I have fitted it with very heavy, wide and puncture-resistant road tyres – my favourites are Schwalbe Marathon Plus. They have less rolling resistance than knobbly off-road-specific tyres, and I find them far less prone to puncturing than knobblies. Punctures not only involve stopping and messing about to replace the inner tube, but in bad conditions they can also result in your body cooling a lot, which is unpleasant at best and at worst potentially dangerous. The grip on these heavy-duty road tyres isn't as good as an off-road tyre's, but I'm not after performance, I'm after dependability. Less grip just means taking corners a little more slowly and losing traction uphill on loose surfaces. If you get wheel-spin going uphill don't fight it, just get off and walk a bit. It gives you a chance to catch your breath and take in the view.

But a cyclo-cross bike, even fitted with off-road tyres, is not the best bike for every ride I've suggested in *Really Wild Cycling*. Some are better done on a bike with off-road tyres that have good grip, and some really rough rides would be better done on a bike with at least front suspension. That means some are best suited to mountain bikes – there aren't many, and I've indicated in the text which ones they are.

You can also reduce punctures by checking your tyres regularly.

Certainly check them at the first opportunity after you've done any wild cycling. Tyres can get cut while riding on trails, or pick up tiny bits of sharp rock or thorns that embed in the tyre. They might not cause a puncture straight away, but they will. Tyre treads and walls are far more robust than they used to be, but you should still replace any tyre that is cut or has been penetrated in any way, even if the penetration isn't deep. Not doing so means the tyre will let you down eventually, and you can bet that will be at the worst possible moment.

Checking tyres for wear is also crucial. You must replace worn, scuffed or bulging tyres. Clean your bike regularly, and whenever you do check the bike's frame and parts for cracks and dents. Anything cracked will eventually fail, so get it replaced. For dents you should get the opinion of a qualified bicycle mechanic, who should be able to asses if it might compromise the bike's safety.

On the subject of bike mechanics, some people love it and are skilled at it, but not everybody. If you'd like to become skilled at maintaining your bike there are plenty of maintenance courses and some good books on the subject. On the other hand, if you are not into bike mechanics take your bike to a shop with a good reputation, and have it service your bike regularly. One thing you should learn to do yourself, because it's something you must do on

a regular basis, is clean and maintain your bike's drive train.

The drive train is the bike's cranks, chainrings, chain and cassette. These moving parts collect grit and dirt while riding, especially when riding off-road and/or in wet conditions, and if grit and dirt are allowed to stay on them they combine with lubricant to create a very effective grinding paste which grinds down the components of the drive train so they wear out quickly. So essential drive-train maintenance involves regular cleaning, then lubrication, of all those parts. It's quite simple to do, and once you get used to it it's a quick job.

First, clean the chain, chainrings and sprockets of any old lubricant and grit or dirt. Use hot soapy water or some form of de-greasing agent. A stiff brush helps you work the water or de-greaser into all the hard-to-reach bits, like between chain links and in between sprocket teeth on the cassette. Once you've cleaned off all the muck and old lubricant, rinse off the soapy water or de-greaser with plain water, then dry the parts thoroughly with an old cloth. Let them air-dry for a bit as well, before applying new bicycle-specific lubricant to the chain. You can get different sorts: light lubricant for summer and heavier for winter.

There are a few skills required for off-road riding that will keep you safe and increase enjoyment. You should certainly learn and practise them if

you want to follow some of the tougher off-road rides in this book. I went over the skills in detail in *Wild Cycling*, so I'm not going to repeat them in detail here. If you aren't confident with riding your bike over rough surfaces, hopping it over low obstacles, riding over low drop-offs, cornering on loose gravel or riding through mud or sand, then I suggest you buy a copy. You can also take courses in off-road cycling skills, and off-road cycling magazines often contain features about riding skills and how to improve them.

The key skill – the one all others follow from, really – is trail reading. The biggest thing to master is focusing on *where you want to go*, not what you want to *avoid* riding through or hitting. When you come to a bit of challenging trail it's worth stopping to pick the best line, which means the smoothest and surest route through it. Then focus on that and nothing else, while coaxing your bike rather than bullying it along the line.

The smoothest line on many tracks is right over to one side or the other, away from the middle. Tracks often get worn into concave grooves, so keeping to one side of a groove will mean riding high up a camber while gravity wants to pull your bike downwards. Counteract this by leaning slightly towards the side you want to stay on, and pushing slightly harder on your outside pedal, to help push you back up where you need to be.

Sometimes it's necessary to cross the section of trail you'd rather avoid, like a patch of deep mud or sand, or an extra-bumpy or loose surface. Pick the smoothest part to cross and head straight over it; don't try to turn or brake while riding through. Get out of the saddle, stay loose, keep your weight spread evenly over your bike and let the bike move up and down underneath you, flexing your arms and legs to absorb the bumps and shocks. After a while you'll develop a sort of split screen in your mind, whereby you're constantly assessing what is ahead and picking the correct line through it, at the same time as coping with the effect the trail you're on is having on your bike.

Understanding the physics of how your bike works helps you a lot with any kind of cycling, but it's crucial when riding off-road. Weight distribution needs to be changed, often constantly, to help maintain control. Un-weighted wheels don't grip like they should, so most of the time when riding on the road or along an even trail you want your weight distributed equally between the front and rear wheels. That's not the case riding on rough trails, where small changes in weight distribution are often required to maintain wheel traction when braking, climbing, descending and cornering.

There are two circumstances that require quite big shifts in body-weight distribution and where your centre of balance is relative to your bike. One is going down very steep hills, when you should keep your backside hovering above and behind the saddle. This is because the angle of your bike means that if you stay in the saddle your weight is distributed much more over the front wheel. That makes any rear-wheel braking less effective than it would be if you were riding on the flat, while front-wheel braking, though more effective, could pitch you over the handlebars. Shift your backside behind the saddle when negotiating very steep off-road descents, therefore, adjusting how far behind to the angle of the descent.

The other big weight shift is required when riding uphill out of the saddle on loose or wet surfaces, both of which compromise traction. To counteract this you need to have your weight back further than you would on a surface with good grip, like a road. Ride out of the saddle uphill as you would on the road on loose surfaces, and your unweighted back wheel could spin.

These are some of the basic skills you will need for the rides in *Really Wild Cycling*, and to plan and follow your own so you can explore, challenge yourself, and enjoy our wild country-side. I hope doing so inspires you as it does me. No matter how long I do it I get great joy from riding my bike. There is a pleasure simply in pedalling, in moving quickly and efficiently under your own power over all kinds of terrain while leaving little trace that you passed by. I look forward to doing so for many years to come. People come and go, but a bike is a friend forever.

1 AROUND YOUR TOWN
A model for riding around the margins of any town, city or other built-up area

WILDNESS RATING **VARIABLE** HARDNESS RATING **VARIABLE**

This first ride embodies the spirit of this book. Riding around the town or city you live in or nearby by linking bridleways and trails, and adding some back roads where there is no off-road alternative, is as enjoyable in planning as it is in execution.

Some of the rides to come are particular challenges, where the fun of doing them is following a geographical line, or overcoming obstacles like mountains, or testing yourself on a classic route that many others have challenged themselves on before. Others are introductions to the wild-cycling possibilities of different parts of the country, and can be varied according to the reader's needs and desires. But a large part of what *Really Wild Cycling* is about is getting out the maps and putting together a ride for yourself – for example, Around Your Town.

I recommend you use Ordnance Survey 1: 50,000 Landranger maps with all the routes, either for reference to check the terrain they cross in detail, or to invent your own short cuts or even add extra loops, as in the case of Ride 1.

I chose riding around the outskirts of a town or city for a couple of reasons. First, it's a nice thing to do, and I'm not the only one who thinks so. Many towns and cities have marked up around-town circuits. In the region where I live the Barnsley Boundary Walk is a long-distance footpath, and the annual Round Rotherham Run is a 50-mile trail race around the boundaries of the South Yorkshire town. The other reason is because it's a great exercise in route-planning with maps. The built-up area is a fixed feature to navigate, whose shape varies as you go, so there will be awkward bits to negotiate and compromises to be

FACT FILE

Where Doncaster in South Yorkshire	**Ride distance** 56 kilometres (35 miles)
Start/Finish Hurst Lane layby A638	**Highest points** Balby 41 metres
OS reference SK 638 985	

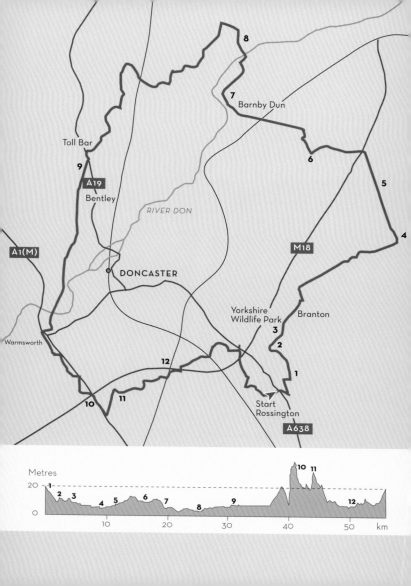

8

7
Barnby Dun

Toll Bar

9

A19

Bentley

RIVER DON

6

5

4

A1(M)

M18

DONCASTER

Yorkshire
Wildlife Park

Branton

3

Warmsworth

2

1

12

10

11

Start
Rossington

A638

Metres

20

1

2

3

4 **5** **6** **7**

8

9

10 **11**

12

0

10   20   30   40   50   km

MAP KEY

1 Hayfield Lakes
2 Railbridge crossing by road
3 Yorkshire Wildlife Park
4 Short stretch of A614

5 Northern Radar Building
6 Turn right off A18
7 Right onto road
8 Kirk Bramwith, follow trans Pennine Trail signs

9 Follow old rail line
10 Under A1(M) junction
11 Loversall
12 Potteric Carr

made. Around-town routes test your eye for picking a line, your technical ability to plan with a map, and your route-finding and -following ability once on your bike.

My first task was to find a place to start and finish near where I live, which is on the south side of Doncaster. The start had to have access to the first trail or back road, which in my case was a bridleway. From there I traced a route on my map right around the outside of Doncaster using as many bridleways as possible, and linking them with sections of quiet roads and a section of the Trans-Pennine Trail.

My start was a lay-by on the A638 just east of Rossington, from where I headed north on the bridleway next to the lay-by. Follow this past Hayfield Lakes to an unclassified road running between Rossington Bridge and Cantley crossroads. Turn right, ride over the rail bridge, then go immediately right onto a bridleway. This is quite bumpy at first but smoothes out through Yorkshire Wildlife Park – sadly, you can't see any of the animals; they are safely behind thick wooden and steel fences.

Continue straight through Branton, crossing the main road and following a minor one to a T-junction. Turn right down Gateforth Lane. This road section was necessary to get to the next set of trails around Armthorpe, which adjoins Doncaster, so at the planning stage I decided it was part of the Doncaster conurbation. I stuck to that rule throughout this ride. Well, almost: on the west side of Doncaster I did slice through Balby, which is joined to the town in a single built-up area. You're allowed to do that once or twice in an exercise like this, I figured.

Eventually you emerge from the bridleway at the A614. Turn left and ride 100 metres looking for the next bridleway that spears off on your left. This goes dead straight north-west for 3 kilometres. On your right you pass the back of the former Northern Radar installation, which from 1946 to 1980 was part of a nationwide tracking service for both military and civil aviation. You can just see the tower the revolving radar head was mounted on. Passing it always takes me back to childhood trips to the seaside: the A614 was the way we went to Bridlington, and when we passed the radar tower, which was working in those days, my dad used to say it was looking for alien spaceships. He said a lot of things, did my dad.

The next section is mostly narrow country lanes. Go left in West End, then left on the A18 for 300 metres, then right opposite a large house. After 800 metres this back road becomes a bridleway: follow it to Barnby Dun. Turn right on the road and follow it through Kirk Bramwith, where you pick up the Trans-Pennine Trail – look for the road sign indicating it on your right.

There are three waterways on this section: the Stainforth and Keadby Canal, the River Don and the New Junction Canal. The two canals are wider than most in the UK because they were used by wider barges that served the South Yorkshire coalfield, bringing in wood for pit props from the port of Goole and taking coal back out to it.

The Trans-Pennine Trail will be referred to a few times in this book; for this section follow the trail signs, which take you first along the trackbed of an old railway, then over a mix of spidery back roads, trails and bridleway. It takes you first through the countryside to a place on the A19 called Toll Bar. Here the Trans-Pennine Trail does a sharp left, initially into a small country park; then, after 100 metres, you go right under the A19 and continue following the old railway line around the back of Bentley, an old mining town just north of Doncaster and separated from it by the River Don.

Continue following the old rail line south-west towards the A1(M) motorway and cross the River Don on an old viaduct. There's a short, steep climb now as the railway line meets a narrow road at the north end of another Doncaster suburb, Balby. Follow this road sharp right, crossing a

bridge over a deep railway cutting, then go second left and follow Church Lane. Then go right on Waverley Avenue and around a playground in the middle of it. Waverley Avenue joins the very busy Warmsworth Road dual-carriageway: cross Warmsworth Road and follow Warde Avenue to Springwell Lane.

Go right on Springwell Lane. Eventually it bends 90 degrees to the right to become Broomhouse Lane and head for New Edlington, but Springwell Lane itself carries straight on, and you should stay on it, heading almost due south. Follow this road as it passes under the multi-layered M18

and A1(M) junction, and continue uphill to the A60. Go left on the A60 and ride for a kilometre to where it begins to bend left. Here you go straight on and follow a small road into the village of Loversall – take great care with this manoeuvre, which is effectively a right turn, so you must signal your intentions to other road users. Keep looking behind and wait for a good gap in traffic before you leave the A60. It's not a massively busy road, but this point is at the end of a long straight stretch and cars tend to go fast along it.

In Loversall take the first right into Rakes Lane, which is a narrow back lane to Loversall Hall. Beyond the Hall Rakes Lane becomes a trail that crosses Loversall Carr. Head for the

massive Amazon building. The Carr – the name for land that is somewhere between marsh and heath – has been landscaped, with many attractive lakes created. It's actually a nice cycling amenity nowadays, with lots of trails for family bike rides.

Look for a bridge over the railway line; cross it and ride around the north end of the Amazon building, heading east alongside the Doncaster and Sheffield Airport Link Road. You then go north through a short tunnel under the Link Road. Turn right immediately, then left through another short tunnel; this one runs under the M18. Yes, this bit of the ride is a bit modern and noisy, but that's about to change.

Once out of the second tunnel you

are in Potteric Carr, which has been preserved as nature intended and is now a nature reserve, home to some rare plants and butterflies. There are a number of ways across Potteric Carr, but they all lead north-east to a footbridge, which requires you to carry your bike up and down two quite long flights of steps. Once off the bridge continue north-east, crossing another railway line by an ungated level crossing. It's not a busy line, but take care here. Stop and look both ways before you cross the railway lines.

You emerge into Carr Lane, in a housing estate. Follow it to Bessacarr Lane and go right. Bessacarr Lane leads to another ungated level crossing and a bridleway. Cross the railway

tracks, taking care again, and follow the bridleway east. After 800 metres it joins a footpath. Dismount, go left and walk up the footpath for 50 metres. This brings you out on the A638, the former Great North Road.

The main road is quite busy, so most local cyclists use the footpath/cycleway that runs in front of the houses on the opposite side of the road. Where you emerge from the footpath, cross the A638 and go right. This footpath/cycleway will take you back to the lay-by you started this ride from.

So there is a ride around my town using bridleways and quiet back lanes, going near as little busy road as possible. Get the OS map out and plan a similar ride around yours.

2

South and South-west of England

2 THE DOWNS LINK

A delightful route connecting the North and South Downs, running from Guildford to the coast. The challenge is doing it all in one go

WILDNESS RATING **4/10**   HARDNESS RATING **4/10**

This linear route follows the trackbeds of two former railway lines. As a place-to-place ride it can be done in either direction, but there is something special about a bike ride to the seaside. The anticipation, the steady change of light as the sea approaches, the moment you smell its glorious salt tang – all this spurs you on and heightens the enjoyment. The other attraction of this ride is the varying ecologies and landscapes it passes through.

The variations are due to the ride's underlying geology. The Downs Link crosses the remnants of the Wealden Dome, which took shape 25 million years ago when a succession of rock layers rose above the sea to form a dome. Over time the dome was eroded, exposing the different bands of rock within it. The type of underlying rock has a big effect on what grows and lives above it, and on the nature of the landscape.

The best place to start this ride is St Martha's Hill above Guildford in Surrey. The hill is part of the Greensand Ridge, which typically has acid soils, so the dominant tree species here are oak, hazel and ash. The North Downs are an attractive, quite heavily wooded area at any time of the year, but this is an amazing place in the spring, when the woodland floors are lit by millions of bluebells.

The direction signs on the Downs Link are quite good, and there are maps you can download from a number of

FACT FILE

Where Surrey to Sussex, finishing on the south coast between Worthing and Brighton

Start St Martha's Hill, Guildford

OS reference TQ 028 483

Finish Shoreham-by-Sea

OS reference TQ 210 054

Ride distance 59.2 kilometres (37 miles)

Highest points St Martha's Hill, 168 metres (551 feet)

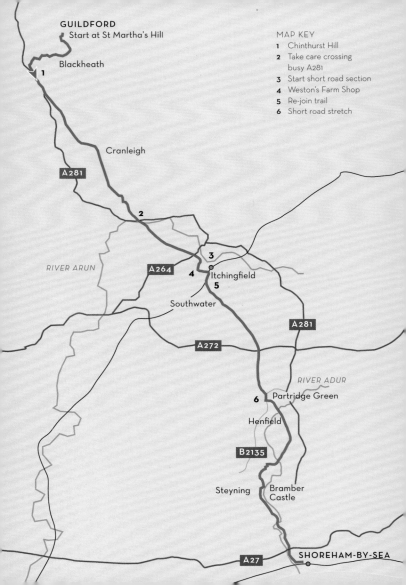

GUILDFORD
Start at St Martha's Hill

Blackheath

1

Cranleigh

A281

2

RIVER ARUN

A264

4

3

Itchingfield

5

Southwater

A272

RIVER ADUR

6   Partridge Green

Henfield

B2135

Steyning   Bramber
Castle

A27   SHOREHAM-BY-SEA

MAP KEY
1   Chinthurst Hill
2   Take care crossing
    busy A281
3   Start short road section
4   Weston's Farm Shop
5   Re-join trail
6   Short road stretch

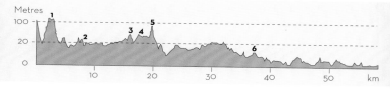

THE DOWNS LINK
Track Elevation

websites including www.wstsussex.gov.uk. The first section of the route passes through woodland, then over a more open area called Blackheath. It's one of the areas of protected heathland in Surrey – a lot of the county's open wild spaces like this have been lost to development and farming.

From running in a south-westerly direction the Downs Link switches south-east after Chinthurst Hill. Following the trail is straightforward, and the surface is generally good, and although the route undulates throughout its journey there are no really steep hills.

The challenge of this ride is in its distance, 37 miles, but, having said that, it is still one of the least challenging rides in *Really Wild Cycling*. That makes it a great one to do if you are quite new to wild cycling and want to try your first longer place-to-place ride.

Twenty-two miles in and the trail crosses the A281, which is a busy road, so take care. There's a short road section just after the route passes

under the A264. You leave the old railway line at the next road bridge after the A264: turn right over the bridge then left at the next junction. Take the first left after Weston's Farm Shop, ride across the bridge over an active railway line, then go first right and look for the trail sign on your right to re-join the Downs Link route.

The next point of interest is Southwater Country Park. It's a former clay-pit, restored and developed into a natural wildlife haven by Horsham District Council. There's a café in the visitor centre if you fancy a quick break, but it's only open at weekends and during school holidays.

Past West Grinstead there is another short stretch of road, the B2135, at Partridge Green. Follow it south for 500 metres, then go left into Homelands Farm, but after 100 metres turn right to re-join the trail.

The countryside is really open now, and the trail continues across the wide shallow valley of the River Adur. Follow the river bank south, where the waymarked route joins suburban roads

As you approach Shoreham the impressive buildings of Lancing College come into view over the river and just north of Shoreham Airport. Built in 1910, Shoreham was the first civil airport in the world.

through Steyning. This section is a bit complicated; take it slowly and look for the route signs.

You pass Bramber Castle in Steyning. It was built in 1070 as part of the Norman Conquest to protect the town, which was then an important river port. Continue on the trail, which follows the Adur even more closely. You should be able to see the South Downs clearly now. Botolphs is where the Downs Link crosses the South Downs Way.

As you approach Shoreham the impressive buildings of Lancing College come into view over the river and just north of Shoreham Airport. Built in 1910, Shoreham was the first civil airport in the world.

Ride under the noisy A27; then you pass an old toll bridge, which was built in 1781 to replace the ferry service across the Adur. Carry on into Shoreham-by-Sea, where you meet National Cycle Network route 2. Enjoy the seaside. There is a railway station in Shoreham, and others just to the east in Brighton and west in Worthing.

3 THE SOUTH DOWNS TRAVERSE

Following the classic route across the entire upland area of the South Downs

WILDNESS RATING **7/10** HARDNESS RATING **9/10**

The South Downs are a chalk upland area in southern England that runs parallel to the English Channel. They rise out of Winchester in the west, and continue east to Eastbourne, a distance of 120 kilometres (75 miles) as the crow flies. This ride follows the South Downs Way cycle trail, which is 160 kilometres (100 miles) long. It's a tough ride – there is very little that's flat about the South Downs! – but a rewarding one through stunning countryside with fabulous views.

You can break the South Downs Traverse into sections, taking as long as you like to complete the whole thing. However, the challenge is to ride all 110 miles of it in a single day. It's a fantastic achievement requiring supreme fitness, good planning and skill. Having said that, only a few brave, hardy and super-fit souls have done the South Downs Double.

The Double is the South Downs Traverse both ways, 220 miles there and back, inside twenty-four hours. There's a fascinating website dedicated to it, www.south downsdouble.co.uk, telling the history of the challenge. It's a valuable resource, indeed, for anyone who wants to follow the South Downs Way by bike, either in stages or all in one go.

Not only does www.southdowns double.co.uk carry detailed maps, but it also has downloadable GPS files of the route. Unless you really love stopping to look at maps, and are good at reading them, a GPS device is almost essential for this ride.

There's a lot of other really useful information the website, even down to where there are public water taps (ten of them, with OS grid references given,

FACT FILE

Where Hampshire and East Sussex	**OS reference** TV 601 984
Start (west-to-east traverse): Winchester	**Ride distance** 176 kilometres (110 miles)
OS reference SU 490 291	**Highest points** Butser Hill, 248 metres (813 feet)
Finish (west-to-east traverse) Eastbourne	

so a map is worth taking even if you are using GPS). There are schedules for ambitious South Downs Single or South Downs Double attempts, as well as potted histories of people who have done Doubles. It's an inspirational website and a tremendous resource for anyone doing this ride, whether all at once or in bits.

As a place-to-place ride you can start the South Downs Traverse at whichever end you like, Winchester or Eastbourne. One consideration might be that the climbs are steeper to the west (Winchester) and longer but less steep on the eastern half, so starting in the west gets the toughest half over first.

Whichever way you go, you must follow the South Downs Way 'Riders' Route'. That's the route for cyclists: the South Downs 'Walkers' Route' uses footpaths in some places, and only walkers can use footpaths. When riding off-road cyclists must follow bridleways and other permitted trails. On Ordnance Survey maps bridleways are the long-dashed red lines.

The Double is the South Downs Traverse both ways, 220 miles there and back, inside twenty-four hours. There's a fascinating website dedicated to it.

If you start from the Winchester end you follow the Pilgrims' Trail south-east until it crosses the South Downs Way on Twyford Down. From Eastbourne you pick up the South Downs Way from the A259, on the western edge of the town. There are many good guidebooks to the South Downs Riders' Route, and this website is invaluable: https://www.southdowns.gov.uk/enjoy/cycling/cycle-rides/

Once you gain height, which involves a steep climb from the

THE SOUTH DOWNS TRAVERSE
Track Elevation

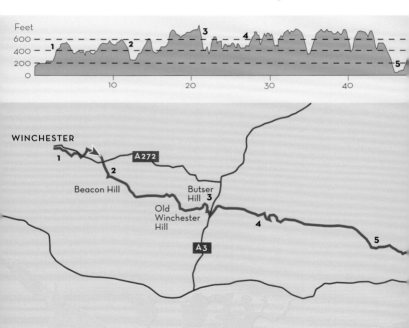

Winchester side but a long, steadier one up a valley from Eastbourne, the trail follows bridleways, tracks and some minor roads. Because they are used by farm vehicles in all weathers the unsurfaced bridleway sections get cut up in the wet. This causes potholes and channels to form, which stay in place when the surface dries. The off-road sections can be very rough in places, and require care and attention to ride over.

That's a characteristic of trails in chalk: they are rock hard in dry conditions, but soft when it's wet. The surface of wet chalk becomes very

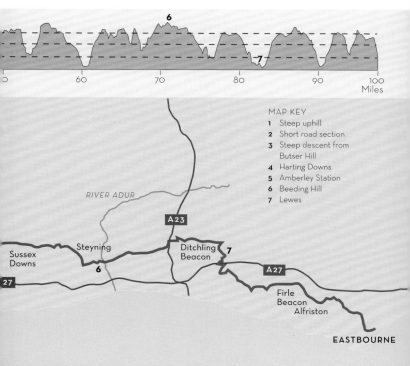

MAP KEY

1 Steep uphill
2 Short road section
3 Steep descent from Butser Hill
4 Harting Downs
5 Amberley Station
6 Beeding Hill
7 Lewes

RIVER ADUR

A23

Steyning

Ditchling Beacon 7

A27

Sussex Downs

27

6

Firle Beacon Alfriston

EASTBOURNE

thin, fluid mud, which is not nice to ride over. Sometimes it's better to ride on the raised centre of trails where grass grows, because it won't be as muddy in the wet.

Old Winchester Hill, just after or before Warnford, is steep in both directions. So is Salt Hill and the climb of Butser Hill if you're doing the ride eastwards. There's a long road section between Queen Elizabeth Park and Harting Downs, which is the start of a long hilly section.

Amberley Station is just over halfway. Going east, it's followed by a long stretch along the northern edge of the South Downs to Botolphs, where you cross the Downs Link, then the River Adur, before the steep climb of Beeding Hill.

There's another long, undulating ridge section between Beeding Hill and Ditchling Beacon, a historic place in cycling because in 1994 the Tour de France climbed the road over Ditchling Beacon on the stage between Dover and Brighton. Then before Lewes (or just after if you are going west) there's a sharp direction shift south.

This sees the South Downs Way cross over the A27 at Housedean Farm for the last leg west over Firle Beacon, through Alfriston and into Eastbourne. Now, how do you fancy turning the bike around and riding back to where you started from?

4 THE RIDGEWAY
A trail ride along part of the UK's oldest road

WILDNESS RATING **6/10** HARDNESS RATING **6/10**

The Ridgeway is one of the oldest roads in the UK. It runs for 87 miles along the northern edge of the central southern chalk downs, from close to Marlborough in Wiltshire to Ivinghoe Beacon, a landmark on the edge of the Chiltern Hills in Buckinghamshire.

The first part of the Ridgeway, from Overton Hill to Streatley, is all bridleway. However, because the way to Overton Hill is heavily used by horse riders, this ride joins the Ridgeway at the next high point along, Hackpen Hill. There are two short road sections at the start and finish, and one more in the middle, but the rest of this ride is off-road trail.

It's lovely: a reasonably long ride with a good feeling of height in places, but not too demanding. Some stretches of the chalk trail are a bit rutted, and the trail is heavier going after prolonged rain. If the weather is fine, though, the ride is a joy and the views are incredible

There's evidence of a track following high ground along the Ridgeway going back at least 5,000 years. Used primarily as a trading route, it linked with other ancient roads to connect the Dorset coast with the North Sea around the Wash.

I've chosen Marlborough in the west to start this Ridgeway ride from, because this way the majority of tough uphill climbing is done early. So, from close to the centre of Marlborough, just outside the church on Kingsbury Street, follow the minor road that Kingsbury Street becomes in a north-westerly direction for 8.7 kilometres to the top of Hackpen Hill.

FACT FILE

Where Wiltshire to Oxfordshire, finishing in the Thames Valley

Start Marlborough

OS reference SU 188 693

Finish Goring-on-Thames

OS reference SU 591 808

Ride distance 62 kilometres (38¾ miles)

Highest point Hackpen Hill (the first: there are two Hackpen Hills on this ride), 268 metres (879 feet)

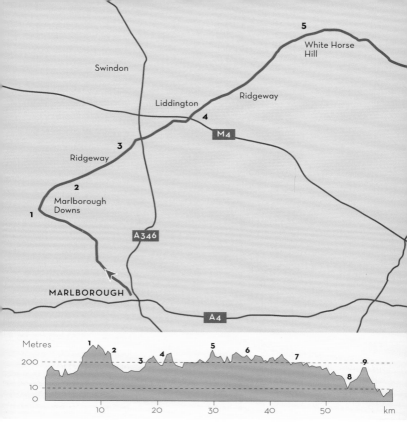

THE RIDGEWAY
Track Elevation

MAP KEY

1   Hackpen Hill.
    Right turn onto trail
2   Barbury Castle
3   Chiseldown
4   Leave road and climb
    Fox Hill
5   Uffington White Horse
6   Lambourne Downs

7   Right turn onto A338
    then left onto trail after
    100 metres
8   Under A34
9   Thurle Down

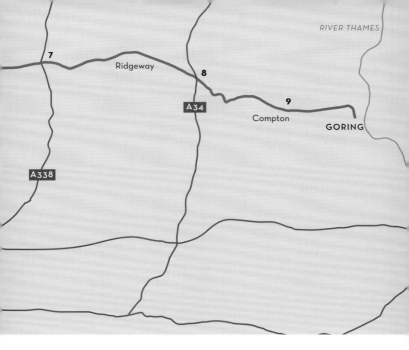

This is a typical escarpment: you climb for almost all of this road section up to the summit, where the land falls steeply away in front of you. Go right here on to the Ridgeway and head north-east.

Marlborough Downs are on your right now, while to the left there is an expansive view across the Vale of the White Horse to Swindon, the white horse in question being the Uffington White Horse, which you will ride close to later on.

The trail is mostly downhill at first,

with a steep descent after Barbury Hill, an Iron Age fort owned today by the National Trust. It's one of many old hill forts along the Ridgeway, all of which helped protect the trade route along it. Later, in the Middle Ages, drovers used this road to move livestock from the west and Wales to markets in and around London.

However, in those days the route of the Ridgeway was open to personal interpretation by travellers, and there were many tracks, some parallel to the line followed today. This changed with

the Enclosures Act of 1750, which blocked most of these tracks, thereby concentrating the movement of people, livestock and goods on the line the Ridgeway follows today. To make the correct path stand out after enclosure, earth banks were built and hedges planted to prevent people or animals straying onto privately owned farmland.

This first long bridleway joins a minor road near Chiseldon, which follows the Ridgeway route and is an example of how, throughout the UK, surfaced roads adopted the paths of bridleways and much older routes.

Just outside Chiseldon you cross the National Cycle Network (NCN) route 45, which at this point runs along the trackbed of an old railway. NCN 45 is a brilliant long-distance route linking Chester with Salisbury, using minor roads, canal towpaths and old railway tracks.

The Ridgeway now slips well below the ridgeline as you pass beneath another former hill fort that was built on Liddington Hill. If you've got the energy to stop on the road and clamber up its slopes, at 277 metres above sea level the summit offers spectacular views. If you want to do other rides in this area a bridleway leads off the summit going south, eventually connecting with a network of other trails you can explore.

Continuing north-east along the Ridgeway you cross Wanborough Plain, passing over the M4 motorway, then taking the first bridleway right. The next section climbs Fox Hill, the route gaining altitude quickly, then becoming quite level for a while. Earthworks and old burial chambers litter this section.

After 7 kilometres of this section you reach White Horse Hill. The Uffington White Horse is on the slope below you now. It is a representation of a horse, 110 metres (360 feet) long, created by removing grass and earth up to a metre's depth to reveal the underlying chalk of the hillside, and could be over 2,000 years old.

The Uffington White Horse can be seen from miles around, and is an incredible sight, as well as a masterpiece of minimalist art and of planning and spatial awareness. The depiction is so precise, so fluid, it's incredible to think ancient people made it. It has always been revered. Local records going back centuries reveal regular scouring ceremonies, in which the surface was cleaned and vegetation removed to keep its edges clear and smooth.

Moving on, you enter an area of gallops used for horse riding, so take extra care. Chalk uplands are perfect for racehorse training, and this section of the ride edges Lambourn Downs, a famous training area.

The direction of the Ridgeway changes now, first to the east, then more south-easterly. The trail also

switches to following the ridgeline again, passing another Hackpen Hill 34 kilometres into the ride, before crossing a minor road at Gramps Hill, then a major one with the A338. Take great care here: you go right onto the main road, then, after 100 metres, the bridleway following the Ridgeway is on your left.

Once you're on the bridleway the route is still rolling, but generally descends as you pass through more gallops country. Keep descending; the Ridgeway passes under the A34 dual-carriageway, then after another 3 kilometres you must turn left at a trail crossroads about 2 kilometres

north of Compton village. You descend a little more, then start the last big climb of this ride to the top of Thurle Down.

It's a steep climb and nearly 2 kilometres long, so a bit of a sting in the tail, but the view from the top in all directions, especially east across the Goring Gap and the River Thames, is worth it. The bridleway you are riding becomes surfaced road at the top of Thurle Down, giving a nice smooth(ish) descent to Streatley. You eventually come to a T-junction: turn right and follow the A329 a few hundred metres to end the ride, which is close to the bridge that joins Streatley with Goring across the Thames.

5 THE TOUR DE TORS
A ride around some of the Tors of Dartmoor

Dartmoor is a wild-cycling paradise, with hundreds of miles of good cycling trails, although you must pay attention to local signs and warning flags, because some parts of it are used for military exercises.

The Tour de Tors is best undertaken on fine days in spring, summer or autumn, because Dartmoor winters can be brutal. On parts of the ride you are a long way from anywhere. It's also better to go for a dry day but, since you will be high up, waterproof clothing should be carried even on fine summer days. The weather can change quickly. Take plenty of food and drink with you too, more than you think you'll need.

Dartmoor is an upland area that welled up as molten lava under the surrounding rock. This rock was subsequently eroded, revealing a vast, undulating dome of granite, punctuated by low rock towers of all shapes and sizes. These are the famous, and characteristic, Dartmoor Tors. This ride links several of these famous landmarks in a fine, airy ride, as well as exploring an old road with a melodramatic name: 'The Way of the Dead' – but more of that later.

Granite tors look a bit like piles of rock slabs, one placed on top of the other. But their slabby look is due to joints in the granite that were created when it cooled from a liquid to a solid state. As it cooled, the granite contracted, which formed open fractures. Hot water moved through the fractures, depositing the minerals quartz and/or tourmaline, which filled the fractures, making them look like joints, quartz being lighter and tourmaline darker than granite.

The ride starts in Peter Tavy, named after the River Tavy running

FACT FILE

Where Mid-Dartmoor, Devon	**Ride distance** 43.2 km (27 miles)
Start and finish Peter Tavy	**Highest point** Conies Down Tor, 502 metres (1,647 feet)
OS reference SX 5143 7762	

Metres

400

200

10   20   30   40   km

THE TOUR DE TORS
Track Elevation

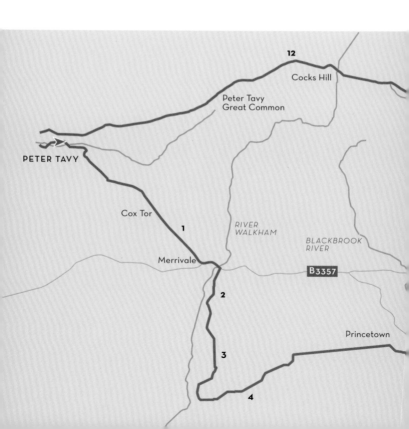

MAP KEY
1 Staple Tor
2 Minor road turns to trail
3 Trail become road again
4 Road to trail transition
5 Left onto road
6 Right onto bridleway
7 Left at bridleway crossing
8 Trail to road transition
9 Right onto bridleway
10 Pine Wood
11 Start of way of the dead
12 Take left bridleway at fork

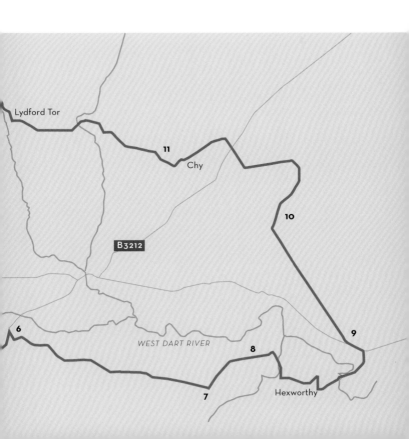

close by the village and its Saint Peter's Church. Head east along the road outside the church, and it quickly becomes steep bridleway as you climb towards Cox Tor. Follow the trail, passing Combs Tor, and then the bridleway, which describes an arc north-east of Cox Tor, eventually leading to Merrivale.

Head east on the road you meet in Merrivale for about 200 metres, then go right on the first bridleway you come to. Go south, past a stone circle and other archaeological sites. There are hundreds, if not thousands, on Dartmoor, and if you want to find more about them then *The Field Archaeology of Dartmoor* by Phil Newman, published by English Heritage, is a good place to start.

This part of the ride follows the boundary between the granite of Dartmoor and surrounding rock, which west of Merrivale has been altered by a process called metamorphosis, whereby the heat from the cooling granite lava concentrates mineral deposits in the rock.

Follow the left side of a valley formed by the River Walkham, and continue south until a minor road, where you go left. The road soon becomes a rough but dead-straight trail, which you follow to Princetown, the site of Dartmoor's famous prison.

The prison was constructed between 1806 and 1809 to hold

captured French soldiers and sailors from the Napoleonic Wars. After them, American prisoners from the 1812 war were locked up there. Conditions were awful: 27 Americans and 1,500 French soldiers died, and in 1815 the institution was closed, only to be reopened in 1850 as a prison for convicted criminals. Various incidents, including several riots, gave HMP Dartmoor a reputation for hardship and as a place to be feared. Its history is documented and very well displayed in a museum located in the prison's old dairy.

From the crossroads in Princeton head north-east towards Two Bridges, then follow the first bridleway on your right, turning left at a bridleway crossing near the River Swincombe. You eventually join a road: follow this through Hexworthy, then north-east over the West Dart river. Turn left at the T-junction, then after 400 metres go right onto a bridleway. The bridleway goes dead straight towards Bellever Tor, then veers right into a delightful pine forest. Follow the bridleway left through the forest, across a clearing, then go right. Cross the B3212 and continue on the bridleway to a tiny settlement called Chy.

From Chy follow the only bridleway west along a natural path across higher ground, passing several granite tors and the remains of ancient settlements along the way. This trail follows the old Lych Way, also known as the Way of

the Dead or the Corpse Way. The scenery is gaunt here, beautifully so in warm sunshine, but austere and wild in any other weather. On those days the trail lives up to its Way of the Dead name. Crossing Dartmoor here in bad weather feels like a sombre death march, but there is a much simpler explanation for the existence of the Lych Way.

The first people to live on Dartmoor, and make a living from it, were farmers in the thirteenth century. They were granted freeholds in the West and East Dart valleys, as well as in the valleys of their tributaries, so long as the freeholders didn't interfere with the King's hunting in the area. Simple terms, but there was a catch. It was a condition of their freehold that these new settlers attended the church in Lydford, the parish covering this part of Dartmoor, for all services and for burials. This could involve carrying a coffin up to 12 miles, and hence the passage was christened the Way of the Dead.

Later on, the farmers asked the Bishop of Exeter if they could attend church at the much closer village of Widecombe-in-the-Moor, and the bishop agreed. However, the Lych Way was preserved for many years because Lydford was the location of the local court, so the West and East Dart farmers still had to go to Lydford to settle all legal matters. This went on until law reforms in the 1800s.

The Lych Way is marked by several examples of Dartmoor Letterboxes. These are part of a game invented by a Dartmoor guide, James Perrott, in 1835. The letterboxes are small stone constructions that contain waterproof boxes with individual rubber stamps in them to identify which box they are from. The game is called letterboxing, and participants carry log books and follow clues to find each letterbox. When they find one, they use the stamp inside to mark their logbooks and prove they have found it.

There are hundreds of such letterboxes scattered all over Dartmoor, and they are often decorated. Many of them along the Lych Way feature macabre etchings of skeletons or coffins. To find out more about letterboxing visit www.dartmoorletterboxing.org.

After 9 kilometres, near the summit of Cocks Hill, the bridleway forks: the Lych Way goes right to Lydford, but you take the left fork that descends across Peter Tavy Great Common, said to be haunted by the ghost of a local man who committed suicide when rejected by the woman he wanted to marry. Six kilometres later you arrive back in Peter Tavy village.

6 DEVON COASTAL HILL-FEST
An exhilarating hill challenge in the breathtaking scenery of North Devon

WILDNESS RATING **6/10** HARDNESS RATING **8/10**

Most of this ride is over surfaced roads, and I make no apologies for that. It is a true wild-cycling experience, as well as a tough physical challenge. In any case, the roads are so tiny, steep and often badly surfaced that they intimidate drivers. Riding this route is a serious cycling feat, and you won't encounter motor vehicles for most of it.

The ride explores the lofty cliffs and narrow valleys between Combe Martin and Woody Bay, as well as the steeply folded countryside behind them. It's a ride for cyclists who like hills, with five distinct climbs that go from almost sea level to at least 250 metres, and adding over 1,400 metres of climbing. That's quite a bit in a distance of 47 kilometres. But none of this ride is flat: it's a very spectacular one with sea views that will take your breath away, exposed sections to

provide a thrill, and deep, secret lush valleys.

Start at the sea end of Combe Martin, sometimes claimed to have the longest single village street in Britain. It doesn't: at 1½ miles from the first house to the last the main street in Combe Martin is certainly long, but there are longer streets in other villages. The main reason for the claim is that until recently it was the only street in Combe Martin. The village occupies a valley so steep-sided there was only room to build along the original road that runs along the bottom of the valley. Nowadays, however, there are offshoot roads in the village because building has taken place up the side of the valley.

After 900 metres of riding you go left on one of these new roads, which climbs steeply up the valley side. It's a brutal introduction to what's to come:

FACT FILE

Where The North Devon Coast	**Ride distance** 47 km (29½ miles)
Start and finish Combe Martin beach	**Highest point** Car park between Holdstone
OS reference SS 7560 4729	Down and Trentishoe Down

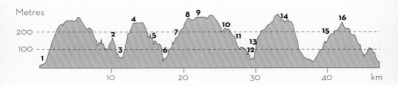

Metres

200

100

1

10 20 30 40 km

DEVON COASTAL HILL-FEST
Track Elevation

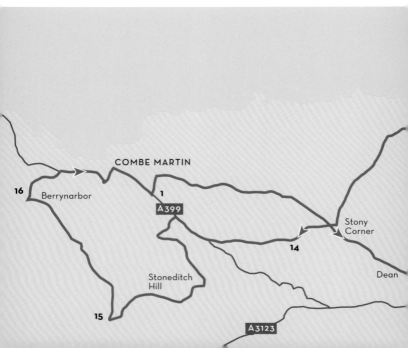

MAP KEY
1 Turn left onto steep road
2 Steep descent
3 Take right fork
4 Right at junction
5 Turn left on outward leg
6 Turn left
7 Turn right at first buildings
8 Turn right at T-junction
9 Turn right just before main road
10 Turn left on return leg
11 Follow bridleway to Killington
12 Turn right on road
13 Steep climb
14 Steep descent
15 Turn right
16 Turn right

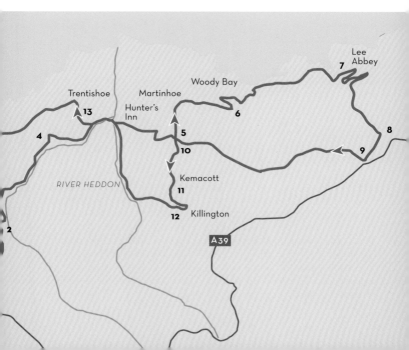

a kilometre of steep climbing up Knapp Down to the top of the valley.

Continue along the valley top, straight over Stony Corner crossroads and down to a hamlet called Dean, where you follow the road left. There's a flat traverse along the edge of a narrow valley, then you descend quite steeply to a fork in the road. Take the right fork and ride past Trentishoe Manor to the T-junction at South Dean Farm.

Turn right to Hunter's Inn, which is in the bottom of the steep-sided River Heddon valley. For an extra adventure there's a bridleway leading north from Hunter's Inn for a kilometre to a tiny beach called Heddon's Mouth, which is a lovely, lonely, secluded spot to visit. For this ride, though, continue east past Hunter's Inn and up the steepest and longest climb of the Devon Coastal

Hill-Fest. It's a real back-breaker: the road gains 200 metres in 1.3 kilometres, which is a 15% average gradient, but with sections of well over 20%.

Catch your breath, then turn left at the crossroads at the top of the climb, continuing through Martinhoe and into the most exhilarating section of this ride. Once you're through the village the view opens up above Woody Bay, and it's amazing. On a clear day you can see right across the Bristol Channel to Wales. You also look down on Woody Bay and its rocky beaches, almost directly below, from what feels like a dizzying height.

Take the next left and descend on a road that clings to the cliff-side. Keep well away from the edge of the road. After a kilometre, just before the second hairpin bend of the descent, there is

another track that corkscrews left down to the beach. Going down is extra to the ride, but a great experience for adventurous and skilful bike handlers. Of course, you'll have to climb back up the same way, and that's not easy.

Once back on the road, continue east up another very steep climb. The road then mostly contours around the headland with incredible views over Lee Bay on your left to Lee Abbey. Go right at the first buildings. A steep climb follows through some woods.

At the second hairpin bend, if you dismount and push your bike east for 300 metres along a path, you get a glimpse of the Valley of the Rocks, a dry flat-bottomed valley that runs parallel with the coast. It is thought to have been the former course of the River Lynn, which after the last Ice Age found

another route into the sea at Lynmouth. Watch out for the wild goats!

Back on your bike, continue up the climb past Sixacre Farm to a T-junction, where you turn right. Turn right again just before the main road and return west to the crossroads above Hunter's Inn. Go left up another steep but quite short hill to Kemacott. Turn left in the village, then right, and continue on a trail that meets a road halfway up a long steep hill. Turn right onto the road and descend to Mill Farm.

You are back in the sylvan glades of the River Heddon valley again. This is another gorgeous section of the ride, a tranquil one after all the exposure of the coast roads. Continue north beneath the trees to Hunter's Inn, turn left at the crossroads and climb to Trentishoe village. Once through the

One of the most interesting buildings is the Pack o' Cards pub on the main street, which was built with the winnings from a card game.

---

village the road climbs steadily to the highest part of this ride, where it passes between Trentishoe and Holdstone Down.

Descend to the main A399, carrying straight on at Stony Corner crossroads. Turn right on the main road, and take the fourth side road on your left, just before a church, which is also on your left. So begins the last climb of the ride.

Keep left at the next junction and climb around Stoneditch Hill to take the second right turn, to Berrynarbor. This section is a long, steady descent, which becomes a steep descent on entering Berrynarbor. Take the first right in the village and climb back up to the junction with the A399 coast road. Turn right and descend to the beach in Combe Martin.

There are lots of interesting things to see in the village. One of the most interesting buildings is the Pack o' Cards pub on the main street, which was built with the winnings from a card game, and its unusual design resembles a pack of cards. And although Combe Martin doesn't have the longest village street in the UK, it is in the *Guinness Book of Records* for hosting the longest ever street party.

7 CORNISH COAST-TO-COAST (AND BACK)
Crossing Cornwall from the Atlantic to the English Channel both ways

WILDNESS RATING 6/10 HARDNESS RATING 5/10

This is one of the easiest rides in the book, but very worthwhile. There is something compelling about riding across a country from coast to coast, so doing it both ways in a day makes this ride very special indeed. And being reasonably easy makes it ideal for someone graduating from short off-the-beaten-track rides to something a bit longer. Plus riding in Cornwall is a delight, especially if the weather is good.

The Cornish Coast-to-Coast links the Atlantic Ocean with the English Channel through a landscape reclaimed by nature, with human help and ingenuity, from the ravages of Cornwall's long-gone mining industry. The landscape is a mixture of natural and industrial heritage, which gives the ride an extra dimension. Old spoil heaps provide extra bone structure for

nature to cover, while old stone chimneys, wheelhouses and other buildings stand as memorials to a way of life that came to an end long ago.

You can start at either end of this one, but I'll describe the route going from Portreath, mainly because it puts the brilliant café at Bissoe at about halfway, so ideal for refuelling. A lot of the route uses the trackbeds of the old tramway network, which linked the tin and copper mines with the two ports that served them. One was Portreath, and the other is our turn-around at the English Channel end, Devoran, which stands on a river flowing into Carrick Roads, the name given to the wide mouth of the River Fal.

The first tin was extracted at Portreath in 1602, and mining grew in its hinterland, quickly replacing

FACT FILE

Where Cornwall	**OS reference** SW 797 390
Start Portreath	**Ride distance** 35.4 kilometres (22 miles) both ways
OS reference SW 655 455	
Finish (or turn-around point) Devoran	**Highest point** Scorrier, 103 metres (338 feet)

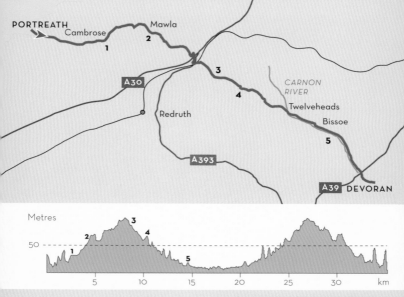

Metres

50 -

5   10   15   20   25   30   km

PORTREATH
Cambrose 1
Mawla 2
A30
Redruth
3
4
CARNON RIVER
Twelveheads
Bissoe
5
A393
A39 DEVORAN

CORNISH COAST-TO-COAST
Track Elevation

MAP KEY

1 Turn left on minor road
2 First bridleway section
3 Follow second bridleway on left
4 Follow trail through Poldice Valley
5 Follow trail past arsenic mine chimney opposite Bissoe Café

agriculture as the main industry of inland Cornwall. In 1809 Cornwall's first railway was built from Portreath to serve copper mines at Scorrier and St Day, but it wasn't just copper and tin that were mined here. Lead, zinc and even gold and arsenic have been mined in Cornwall. The rich veins of metal underground here were created by heat and pressure on surrounding sedimentary rocks by volcanic processes that created the present-day Bodmin Moor.

Start on the harbour wall in Portreath and head inland to pick up the B3300, heading east out of the village. Turn left onto a minor road after 3 kilometres, and ride through Cambrose to Mawla, where opposite a T-junction you'll see the first bridleway section stretching ahead of you. Follow this bridleway to Scorrier, where you double back on a path that joins a bridge. Use this to ride over the A30. Go left at the next T-junction and join the B3298, going south-east for 1 kilometre, then turn left onto the second bridleway on your left.

Lovers of Cornish clotted cream will recognise that the celebrated producer of the cream tea staple, A. E. Rodda and Son, is based in Scorrier.

In 1809 Cornwall's first railway was built from Portreath to serve copper mines at Scorrier and St Day.

The business is over 120 years old, and its products are still made in the same way from top-quality local milk. The characteristic crust on Rodda's clotted cream has a golden tinge because the grass the cows eat is high in a pro-vitamin called beta-carotene. Beta-carotene is thought to make a positive contribution to maintaining good eyesight.

Next comes one of the old tramway sections: part trail, part back roads leading straight south-east into the Poldice Valley. You are right in the heart of the old metal-mining country here – the valley sides would have echoed with the chuffs and whistles of steam power and the clatter of machinery. You pass close to the valley village of Twelveheads, which takes its name from a celebrated ore-crushing steam hammer used at its local processing works.

The valley was carved by the Carnon river, which from a trickle builds to a sizeable stream by the time it gets to Bissoe. Bikechain Bissoe, a café and bike-hire facility, is right next to the trail here. Time to take a break now, or in another 8 kilometres on your way back. The café is full of cycle racing memorabilia, signed racing jerseys and all sorts of interesting stuff.

Arsenic mining was particularly prevalent around this part of the ride. Some of the old buildings of the Point Mills arsenic refinery are just across

Arsenic mining was particularly prevalent around this part of the ride. Some of the old buildings of the Point Mills arsenic refinery are just across the road from Bikechain Bissoe.

the road from Bikechain Bissoe. The Carnon river here was polluted by arsenic, but various schemes have cleaned it up, including reed planting. Certain types of reeds absorb arsenic.

Not far to the turn-around now. Stay on the trail, passing under a viaduct and passing the original stone piers of the first railway viaduct across this valley, one built by Isambard Kingdom Brunel. You eventually get to Devoran, the English Channel port for the metal ore mining industry. Boats were loaded on the quay here, and tin and copper ore was shipped to Falmouth for onward transfer to bigger vessels.

If you are feeling extra-adventurous at this point, follow the coast road running alongside Restronguet Creek to Feock and Retrongouet Point, where the Carnon river joins Carrick Roads. The scenery in this little-known part of Cornwall is stunning.

Whatever you decide, though, Devoran is the start of the return trip on this Cornish Coast-to-Coast ride. You should know the way back by now. Enjoy!

3

Central England

8 CROSSING THE COTSWOLDS
A mixed bridleway and back-road adventure from one side of the Cotswolds Hills to the other

WILDNESS RATING **5/10** HARDNESS RATING **7/10**

The Cotswold Hills run in a widening south-west-to-north-east arc, rising steeply in Gloucestershire at the Cotswold Edge and rolling gently down into Oxfordshire, with the edges of the hills touching other counties on the way. Traversing the Cotswolds roughly follows the orientation of the Cotswolds, starting out quite hilly in Stroud at the Cotswold Edge side and ending with a more rolling passage into Banbury.

The Cotswolds are mostly limestone, which supports a wonderful grassland habitat packed with wild flowers, dotted with woods and glades, while providing the basic construction material, Cotswold stone, for the distinctive Cotswold towns and villages. Most buildings are made from this local limestone, which ranges in shade from bright white through honey tones to light toffee colours.

This is a fairly long ride with a complicated route, and therefore one it's best to get familiar with by plotting it on an Ordnance Survey (OS) map before you ride it. Once you've done that from the directions here, including any little deviations or short-cuts you want to add, you can take the maps with you to consult on the way. More conveniently, though, mapping apps allow you to plot a course on a laptop or other device, then download it to your GPS, so you just follow directions on the GPS screen.

Crossing the Cotswolds uses parts of the Macmillan Way, where this long-distance trail goes across the Cotswolds in its course from Boston in Lincolnshire to Abbotsbury in Dorset. The Macmillan Way is designated as

---

FACT FILE

Where Gloucestershire and Oxfordshire	**Ride distance** 85 kilometres (53 miles)
Start Stroud	**Highest point** Bisley, 240 metres (there are several 230-metre hill tops along the way) (787 feet)
OS reference SO 850 052	
Finish Banbury	
OS reference SP 453 404	

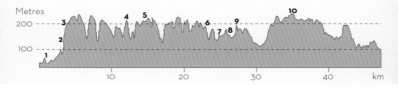

MAP KEY

1 Turn left up old
   neighbourhood
2 Right just before Bisley
3 Follow Macmillan Way
   to Chedworth
4 Follow Monarch's Way
   to Hampnett
5 Follow Macmillan Way
   to Cold Aston
6 Turn right before
   Lower Swell
7 Left onto the Diamond Way
8 Chaselton Barrow Fort
9 Turn right
10 Left to Hook Norton

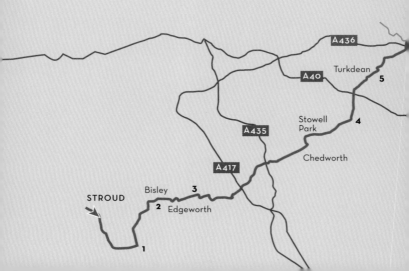

footpath for much of its length, but does have bridleway sections and uses some minor roads in the Cotswolds, so those parts are open to use by cyclists. Check out the website, www.macmillanway.org, for further details of the whole trail.

As well as being a quite long ride with some tough hills thrown in,

Crossing the Cotswolds is a navigational challenge. Those wanting a purely physical challenge might want to try the Hell of the North Cotswolds, an annual organised event that takes place on various routes, the longest being 100 kilometres (62 miles), which starts and finishes in Winchcombe. Also known as HONC, the Hell of the

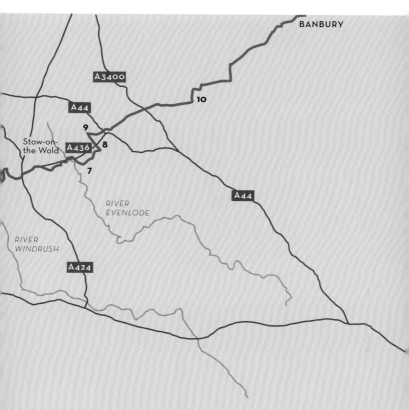

North Cotswolds uses an intricate route, linking back roads with bridleways and a few footpaths. Permission to use the footpath is only granted on the day of the event, so it's impossible to ride all of this splendid route at any other time of the year.

A couple of sections of Crossing the Cotswolds use parts of the HONC route. It starts in Stroud on the western edge of the Cotswolds, which is right on the Cotswold Edge, and going from here in the south-west in a generally north-eastern direction will give you a feel for the underlying processes that created the Cotswold Hills. The Cotswold Edge is evidence of uplifting in the limestone block the hills are made from, representing the point of greatest uplift to create a steep, west-facing slope. The rest of the limestone block dips steadily towards the south and east, although it is by no means downhill, as you dip into and out of several steep-sided stream and river valleys along the way. You'll see the changes as the ride progresses.

Stroud is a vibrant place, well-liked by artists and very attractive with its streets marching in serried ranks up the encroaching hillsides. The hills are cleft by the River Frome which, setting off from a double roundabout in the town centre, you follow along the A419, Dr Newton's Way, going east then south-east. Ride for 6.5 kilometres, then go left at the church and climb up a road called Old Neighbourhood, following this to Bisley. Go right in Bisley on Heyhedge Lane, heading for Edgeworth. This road turns into a trail for a short section through some trees. You descend steeply into the trees, then climb steeply out.

Go through Edgeworth and, heading east, descend into and climb out of another steep-sided valley. Once on level ground turn right, then first left, to follow a bridleway, part of the Macmillan Way. Turn left into Middle Duntisbourne and first right to climb again. Once under the A417 at the top of the hill go immediately left onto a stretch of trail to Woodmancote, following the Macmillan Way through the village.

Cross the A435 with care, then continue north-east through Rendcomb, keeping left to continue on the Macmillan Way to Chedworth, where there is another short steep down-and-up. Continue north-east on a minor road now, through Stowell Park, and go left onto a stretch of the Monarch's Way. Follow the bridleway until it joins a surfaced road in Hampnett and go north, crossing the A40 with great care and following the little lane opposite to Turkdean.

Go through Turkdean and, just as you leave the village going north-east, turn right to pick up the Macmillan Way again. Follow the Macmillan Way

through Cold Aston and turn left just before the A436. Cross the A436 and ride past Aston farm, crossing the River Windrush, which gave its name to the ship, the *Empire Windrush*. In 1948 the *Empire Windrush* brought the first of a generation of people from the West Indies invited to Britain to help rebuild it after the Second World War, who became known as the *Windrush* Generation.

Road switches to bridleway soon after you cross the Windrush. Follow a bridleway that gets quite rough where it crosses open fields, then take a right where the trail forks to cross a minor surfaced road and enter Lower Slaughter. This is an absolutely gorgeous village. The Cotswold Hills are studded with gems like this, but Lower Slaughter is one of its brightest and best. Cross the River Eye and go left past the church, then right at the next junction towards Lower Swell.

Turn right just before the village and head for Hyde Mill, crossing the River Dickler just before you reach the A429. Now, take care, because you go left on the A429 and, as soon as you've done that, start looking on your right for a road entrance that is concealed by trees. It's only 200 metres along the main road. Turn right and follow this road, which is the Macmillan Way through Maugersbury, going right again at the A436 onto the B4450. After a kilometre turn left to ride through Upper and Lower Oddington.

Unfortunately you have another bit of main road now, because it's the only way to get across the River Evenlode. Turn right on the A436, cross the river and take the first right. After a kilometre, and just past New Farm, go left onto a bridleway that is part of the Diamond Way. Turn right at the next road junction, then first left before crossing the A436 and riding past Chastleton Barrow Fort to take the next right. Cross the A44 and follow a bridleway for 500 metres, go right on another bridleway for 200 metres, then go left on the next road.

Carry on straight for 9 kilometres, through Church End, and go left to Hook Norton, then right through the

village, then left to Wiggington Heath, then right to Lower Tadmarton. Go right on the B4035 in Lower Tadmarton and follow this road to the finish of the ride in Banbury.

That's 57½ miles (92 kilometres) across the Cotswolds, from Gloucestershire to Oxfordshire, a glorious ride but a tough one. Banbury is a lovely place, full of history, but

most know it because of the nursery rhyme about riding:

a cock horse to Banbury cross
To see a fine lady upon a white horse.

A cock horse, in the context of the nursery rhyme, was one of two things:

1 Something used as a make-believe horse, such as the knee of an adult or a rocking-horse.

2 A horse added to a team of horses to assist a wagon through high water or over difficult terrain.

The 'fine lady' was believed to be a Fiennes lady, Celia Fiennes (1662–1741), member of a local noble family and an intrepid traveller, and an ancestor of the great adventurer Sir Ranulph Fiennes.

9 ICKLE BIT OF ICKNIELD
A taster of one of England's oldest transport routes

WILDNESS RATING 4/10 HARDNESS RATING 4/10

The Icknield Way is another of the UK's ancient trackways. It is named after the Iceni tribe, a pre-Roman people who lived in the east of England. The Icknield Way starts where the Ridgeway ends, close to Ivinghoe Beacon, and was used in ancient times as a continuation of the link between the west of England and the English Channel and the North Sea.

The Icknield Way Trail runs from Ivinghoe Beacon in Buckinghamshire to just east of Thetford in Norfolk, but completing the whole distance is only for walkers. That's because parts of it are on footpaths, so out of bounds for cyclists. Apart from a short stretch from Buckinghamshire into Bedfordshire, the Icknield Trail cycle route runs from near Luton to Thetford and follows bridleways and some minor roads.

This ride is a sample of that much longer cycle route, which is in excess of 200 kilometres (120 miles). Ickle Bit of Icknield starts in Newmarket and runs to Great Chesterford, which is in Essex and just north-west of Saffron Walden, and it is probably the quietest and prettiest section of the whole Icknield Trail.

This is not a hard ride, although riding both ways would be a good test of stamina, but it provides a good feel for this ancient road, and will maybe whet your appetite for longer rides on this trail, or even for completing the whole thing. If you decide to plan a longer exploration of the Icknield Way Trail, this website is invaluable: www.icknieldwaytrail.org.uk.

FACT FILE

Where From Breckland in Norfolk through Cambridgeshire to north Essex

Start Newmarket, The Guineas shopping centre, Fred Archer Drive

OS reference TL 643 636

Finish Great Chesterford

OS reference TL 505 429

Ride distance 40 km (25 miles)

Highest point Burrough's End, 117 metres (384 feet)

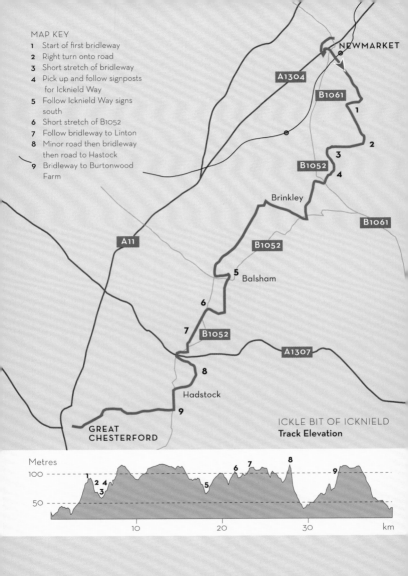

MAP KEY
1 Start of first bridleway
2 Right turn onto road
3 Short stretch of bridleway
4 Pick up and follow signposts
  for Icknield Way
5 Follow Icknield Way signs
  south
6 Short stretch of B1052
7 Follow bridleway to Linton
8 Minor road then bridleway
  then road to Hastock
9 Bridleway to Burtonwood
  Farm

NEWMARKET

A1304
B1061
1
2
3
B1052
4
Brinkley
B1061
B1052
5 Balsham
6
7 B1052
A1307
8
Hadstock
9
A11
GREAT
CHESTERFORD

ICKLE BIT OF ICKNIELD
Track Elevation

Metres
100
50
2 4
3
5
6 7
8
9
1
10   20   30   km

The area around Balsham is said to be haunted by a mythical beast said to have the body of a sheepdog and the face of a monkey.

The Icknield Way is very well signposted. The trail logo is a depiction of a Stone Age tool, a hammer inside a circle, and is on all trail signposts. Each signpost then has qualifications added to it like 'Byway' 'Bridleway' or 'Riders' Route'. Those are the signs you must follow when cycling. Any sign indicating footpath or 'Walkers' Route' is not for cyclists.

Starting outside The Guineas shopping centre head south-east along Fred Archer Drive, turn left into St Mary's Square, then Rowley Drive, and keep riding all the way to the open land of Newmarket Heath. Go left where the road meets the heath and follow the road to its T-junction with the A1304. Go left on the A1304 and ride for half a kilometre, looking for Dullingham Road on your right. Turn right onto Dullingham Road, then carry straight on where this road bends right.

You are now on Woodditton Road. Keep going south-east, then turn right at the staggered junction. After a kilometre the first bridleway section starts on your left, where there is a ' No fly-tipping' sign. The trail sign is slightly hidden by a tree here, so keep a close look-out for it. Follow this bridleway to Ditton Green, where you turn right and follow a minor road until the first sharp-right bend, where the Icknield Way continues straight ahead on a short stretch of bridleway.

By now it's just a question of carefully following the Icknield Way signposts, as the route switches from short stretches of road to bridleway, then back again, all the way to Brinkley. There's a long stretch of well sign-posted bridleway from there to Balsham, which is famous for a Viking raid in 1015, during which only one villager survived. The village is also famous for the Shug Monkey. The area around Balsham is said to be haunted by a mythical beast with the body of a sheepdog and the face of a monkey.

Locally it's called the Shug Monkey, but a similar creature exists in Norse folk tales.

Head east to the centre of Balsham on the B1052, then go right just after the church onto Woodhall Lane. The Icknield Trail continues south, then joins another trail following the course of a Roman road. Turn right and continue along the new trail until the B1052 road, where you go left, then continue straight on a bridleway where the B-road turns sharp left. The bridleway leads to Linton, a village with another myth. The TV character Alan Partridge claims Linton is halfway between London and his home in Norwich, which is why he stays in the village at the fictitious Linton Travel Tavern.

Continuing south out of Linton you have to cross the A1307: take care. On the other side of the road you'll find a lane going left. Follow this lane across the B1052, past a windmill, where the lane becomes bridleway. Follow the bridleway to a minor road where you go right – it's on a bend, so it's straight on, really – to Hadstock.

Turn left in Hadstock onto the B1052 and go south. At the top of the hill look right for a bridleway. Use that bridleway to ride across Hadstock Common, which is heavy going in places, to Burtonwood Farm, where the bridleway becomes a lane. Follow the lane into Great Chesterford and the end of the ride.

10 CRISS-CROSSING THE LONG MYND

How many times can you summit or cross a single hill or mountain, or even a range of hills and mountains, by different routes? At least five on this ride over the Long Mynd in Shropshire

WILDNESS RATING **6/10** HARDNESS RATING **7/10**

The Long Mynd is one of the most impressive of the lovely Shropshire Hills, which lie between the English Midlands and Wales, although they are slightly more Welsh than English in character. Mynd is a Welsh word for mountain, and at 7 miles (11 kilometres) long, to a maximum width of 3 miles (5 kilometres), the Long Mynd is literally a long mountain. With a number of bridleways and back roads crossing its width, the Long Mynd offers an interesting wild-cycling challenge.

It's a simple one, but it requires planning and imagination. How many different routes can you find across one hill, across either the summit or the ridge line of a long, slim hill like the Long Mynd? I found five separate routes across it for this ride, but there are many more. It's a challenge you can set yourself on any long hill or ridge. Mountains really lend themselves to this exercise, although you need experience and excellent fitness to take on really high places.

Crossing Helvellyn in the Lake District by its many bridleways would make a wonderful but extreme wild-cycling challenge.

This ride has quite a bit of road in it, but it's all back roads, and its off-road sections are testing in places. Some are quite rocky, so you need a bike with good off-road-riding capabilities. A mountain bike is best suited, but if you are a good bike handler a cyclo-cross bike works too.

It starts in the village of All Stretton, the most northerly of three settlements with Stretton in their name that lie in the Stretton Gap.

FACT FILE

Where Shropshire

Start and finish All Stretton

OS reference SO 460 955

Ride distance 58 kilometres (36¼ miles)

Highest point Pole Bank, 502 metres (1,647 feet)

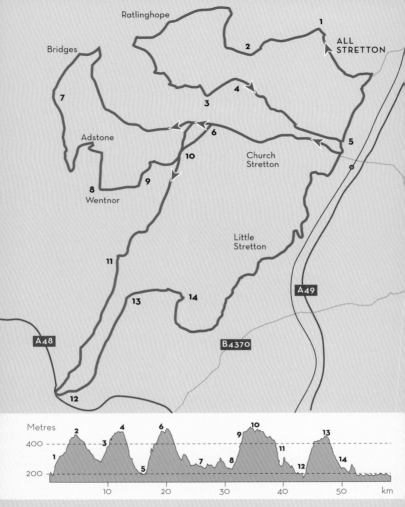

CRISS-CROSSING THE LONG MYND
Track Elevation

MAP KEY

1 Turn left onto bridleway
2 Robin Hood's Butts, follow
   road to Rattling Hope
3 Summit car park, go left
4 Go right onto Mott's Road
   descent
5 Turn right, then right again
   to climb Burway Hill
6 Continue straight after

   Boiling Well, then descend
   to Bridges
7 Take left fork in road
8 Left at T-junction
9 Start of steep uphill trail
   section
10 Continue straight over
   summit of Pole Bank, then
   turn right, then first right to
   double back

11 Very steep descent to
   Asterton
12 Left just before Plowden to
   follow Jack Mytton Way
13 Take first right into summit
   pine plantation
14 Follow trail right fork to
   Hamperley then go left to
   Little Stretton

The Gap lies between the Long Mynd and a succession of other Shropshire Hills. The one opposite All Stretton is called Caer Caradoc, and its steep sides make it a very impressive site. Caer Caradoc is volcanic in origin, and lies on a geological fault that runs from Staffordshire to South Wales.

Start on the B5477 at the bottom of Castle Hill in All Stretton and climb Castle Hill, keeping left. Turn left onto a bridleway after 2.6 kilometres and continue climbing to the next surfaced road. Turn left and continue on the road to a place called Robin Hood's Butts, an ancient burial site and the summit of the first Long Mynd crossing.

Descend on the road to Ratlinghope – watch out for the long, sweeping and quite steep left bend about halfway down. Turn left in Ratlinghope, then take the first left to begin the second crossing of Long Mynd. This is a steep road climb up to a summit car park, where you go left to the high point of another crossing.

The trail splits at the summit, and you go immediately right onto a trail

called Mott's Road. This is a very popular off-road trail with local mountain bikers. It descends steeply, gets quite technical and tricky in places, and it's rocky. There are also some widely spaced step-downs. They aren't deep, and if you are used to handling drop-offs on a bike then they are fine to ride, but if you aren't happy with your skills on trails like this then walk down the steps.

The last part of the trail, before it joins a surfaced road, is very rocky, so again walking is advised if you aren't confident of your bike-handling on rocky terrain. You eventually come to a car park at the top of the Carding Mill Valley road. Continue along the road to Church Stretton.

This is the largest of the Strettons in the Stretton Gap. Follow the road you are on until its T-junction with the B5477. Go right and ride along the B5477 until you see Burway Road on your right; it's at a crossroads. Stay on Burway Road to climb Burway Hill – quite a steep pull in the beginning, but it flattens out for the last 2 kilometres to the summit.

The Burway was an ancient road, and the road you are climbing now follows it. At 492 metres (1,514 feet) the summit is the highest public road in Shropshire, but you carry straight on where it bends left just after a place called the Boiling Well to follow a trail. Carry on to the summit, which is just north of Pole Bank, the highest point on Long Mynd. You'll ride over that later, but for now continue west for the long descent into Bridges. That's the third Long Mynd crossing done.

Bridges is a tiny hamlet in the lovely and very secluded River Onny valley. Turn left as you enter Bridges, then left again just past the houses and ride along this road until it forks. Take the left fork. Keep left, then go left at the T-junction, follow the road right through Adstone and go left at the next crossroads.

As you climb steadily towards the steep west flank of Long Mynd prepare yourself, because the next bit is tough. Turn left at the T-junction, then look for a trail on your right. This climbs diagonally up the west flank, with a kink about halfway to get over a really steep bit. It's a tough one, this, so you might end up walking sections or all of it. It's only for a kilometre in total, though: then the slope relents.

At the top you go left on a road that follows another ancient communication link, the Portway. Turn left onto the road, then, where it forks, with the road going right, you join a track that goes left. Follow the track to the summit of Pole Bank, the highest point on the Long Mynd at 502 metres (1,647 feet). Continue over Pole Bank, turn right at the trail

crossroads, then first right onto a narrow road that follows the path of the Portway.

Follow this road, which at this point also carries the long-distance footpath the Jack Mytton Way, past the gliding club. Then take extra care: the road flicks right, then descends very steeply to Asterton. Keep your speed in check on this section. Turn left in Asterton and follow the road around the pointed end of Long Mynd. Look for the Jack Mytton Way sign just before Plowden.

Turn left onto the Jack Mytton Way – it shares a course with the Shropshire Way at this point – and start climbing the bridleway up the centre line of Long Mynd. It's a hard slog to the summit, one for low gears and strong legs, but the view at the top is fantastic. On a clear day you can see the mountains of Wales in the west, some days even as far as the Brecon Beacons.

At the summit there's a pine plantation on your right: look for a bridleway that spears off to the right at 45 degrees to the Jack Mytton Way. Turn right onto the bridleway and descend through the pine plantation. This is a lovely fire-road descent that joins a surfaced road near the bottom leading to Hamperley.

Turn left in Hamperley and ride to Little Stretton, then go left there onto the B5477 and follow this road back to All Stretton. That's five crossings of Long Mynd done in a fairly strenuous 58 kilometres, but it's possible to do a lot more crossings on this hill, if you have the time and the stamina.

11 RAGGED STAFF
Celebrating the adventurous spirit of cyclists from another time

WILDNESS RATING **6/10** HARDNESS RATING **6/10**

This ride celebrates a wild-cycling movement from years ago, and one of the biggest flag-wavers for cycling off the beaten track from the same era.

His name was Rex Coley, and this ride is a challenge picked especially for people who enjoy riding the classic steel bikes of yesteryear. Coley was a cyclist and a writer who worked for a British magazine called *Cycling*, often writing under his pen-name, Ragged Staff, a reference to the bear-and-ragged-staff coat of arms of his native Warwickshire.

Coley's passion was cycle-touring, which he wrote about with deep affection in two books whose titles shout out their contents: *Cycling is Such Fun* (1947) and *Joyous Cycling* (1953). The latter had a foreword by the multi-world sprint champion, Reg Harris. Harris was a track racer, the

fastest man in the world over the sprint distances in the late 1940s and early 1950s, but cycle-touring was his lifelong hobby. He started his cycling life with the Bury branch of the Cyclists' Touring Club (CTC), a body now known as UK Cycling, and continued to enjoy cycling in the Cheshire countryside right up to his death.

A common thread ran through all Coley's work: the joy of cycling just for its own sake. He loved exploring on his bike, seeking out off-the-beaten-track routes, the wilder the better. Coley started to champion this kind of cycling in print during the 1950s, because he felt that cycle racing had developed in Britain at the expense of the club runs, the gentle rides and cycle touring he loved. He wasn't alone: a body called the Rough Stuff Fellowship formed in 1955, its members' objective being to preserve

FACT FILE

Where Derbyshire's Peak District	**Ride distance** 60 kilometres (37½miles)
Start and finish Black Rock, near Wirksworth	**Highest point** Parsley Hay, 350 metres (1,148 feet)
OS reference SK 292 557	

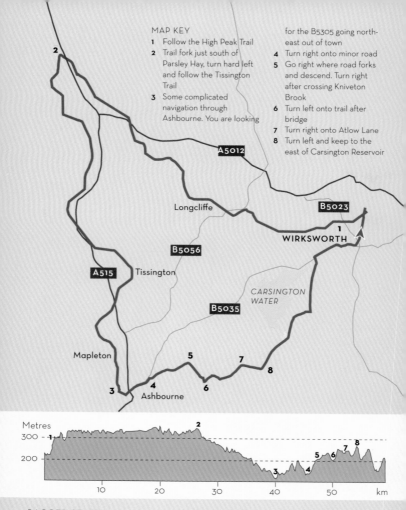

MAP KEY

1. Follow the High Peak Trail
2. Trail fork just south of Parsley Hay, turn hard left and follow the Tissington Trail
3. Some complicated navigation through Ashbourne. You are looking for the B5305 going north-east out of town
4. Turn right onto minor road
5. Go right where road forks and descend. Turn right after crossing Kniveton Brook
6. Turn left onto trail after bridge
7. Turn right onto Atlow Lane
8. Turn left and keep to the east of Carsington Reservoir

A5012

Longcliffe

B5023

WIRKSWORTH

B5056

A515 Tissington

CARSINGTON WATER

B5035

Mapleton

Ashbourne

Metres

300

200

10 20 30 40 50 km

RAGGED STAFF
Track Elevation

the spirit of using bikes for pleasure and adventure, and not just as tools for transport or competition.

The joy of exploring by bike is growing in appeal again, and not just among cyclists who use modern bikes to go off-grid and explore trails, bridleways and roads less travelled, but with enthusiasts who renovate old steel bikes, or buy renovations from a growing number of providers.

Many use such bikes to get off the beaten track and explore the countryside, just like they did on the old days. This ride respects the spirit of exploration handed down from Coley and the members of the Rough Stuff Fellowship, while celebrating the beauty of steel bikes from another age.

The ride I picked is one that Coley would have loved, and one well suited to riding on a classic steel bike. With their chrome details and vibrant enamel, old steel bikes are iconoclasts in the corporate world of modern cycling. The most celebrated brands were created for form as well as function, often by artists working alone or with small teams of craftsmen. This resulted in individual creations, whereas today's race bikes are more about speed and efficiency, to which there are common solutions, so their designs end up being quite similar. With a few exceptions the colour palette of modern bikes is more muted too.

There is one drawback to old steel bikes, especially old steel race bikes: they don't have a wide range of gears, and the number of ratios you can select is limited. This can restrict the gradients that can be tackled on them, at least without making huge efforts. Just look at old film of the Tour de France and other big races: on mountain roads the riders' pedal revs were much lower than they are today, and they had to get out of the saddle and really muscle their bikes up the steepest bits. It's a historic fact that the really steep passes we see in top-level racing today, like the Zoncolan in Italy or the Alto de L'Angliru in Spain, were opened up to cycle racing after race-bike design evolved to allow lower, and a wider range of, gear ratios.

On top of that, the increased sophistication of modern off-road bikes opens a wider range of terrain for more people to ride. It is possible to take on some pretty gnarly terrain on an old steel bike – footage on the Internet of old cyclo-cross races shows that – but only if you're very fit and very skilful. Modern cyclo-cross, and in particular mountain bikes with their sophisticated suspension systems, make light work of terrain that once could only be negotiated by the gifted, and even then sometimes on foot.

The Ragged Staff ride is set in the southern part of the Peak District, the White Peak, home of the retro cycling festival Eroica Britannia and a mecca for steel-bike enthusiasts who ride the long, specially prepared cycle trails here. It's a hilly area, but the trails

follow old railway trackbeds, so the steepest ups and downs were engineered out when the railways were built. There are still hills in this ride, though: one or two unavoidable pulls on the trails, and the final third of the ride is quite undulating. As ever in this

part of the country, the scenery compensates for any extra effort.

You start and finish at a place called Black Rock, just outside of Wirksworth. There's a small car park at Black Rock, and it's an ideal place from which to access the first trail, the High Peak Trail. Navigation is fairly straightforward on this ride: the only instruction for the first 20 kilometres is simply to follow the High Peak Trail westwards at first, then north-westwards.

The prepared trails here are often

dressed with crushed limestone, and they are lovely to ride on. You hardly notice the surface, so you fully engage with the scenery. The trail hovers around the 300-metre contour line, and it feels high up here, with a big open sky above you. You can see for miles over a limestone landscape with few trees but acres of grassland, grass a shade of green only limestone supports. The White Peak is a wonderful place imbued with light and a feeling of freedom. Larks sing, buzzards soar and swifts squeal around isolated barns and the stone houses of villages like Longcliffe.

You cross the A5012, ride past Friden Works, then under the busy A515, then go another 800 metres until you reach a trail fork. You've just ridden up one prong of the fork; now you switch directions, turning hard left to ride down the other prong, so you are heading south. This is the Tissington Trail, and you follow it all the way to Ashbourne. Good news: this bit is mostly downhill.

Turn left at the first surfaced road just outside Ashbourne, called Mapleton Road, and head into town. Go right into Dovehouse Green, then left into Union Street. Turn left onto the A515 from Union Street and head north for about 50 metres, then go right onto King Street. This the B5035. Follow it out of Ashbourne going north-east until it bends left. Take the second right here and follow a minor

road, still heading north-east, until it forks after a steep dip down into and out of a small valley.

Take the right fork, Kniveton Lane, and descend into another steep-sided valley. Turn right just after crossing the little bridge, then go left onto Ridge Lane. Continue past the solar farm, then turn left and almost immediately right onto Atlow Lane. Follow this road until you go under some electric wires, and turn left onto Brick Kiln Lane.

Follow this road, and go left, then right at the next junction. Continue along Gibfield Lane, then fork left onto Broom Lane, then Benthead Lane, then Blind Lane. You should be able to see Carsington Water on your left now. You end up at a crossroads in Moorside: go left and follow this road all the way to the B5035. Turn right onto the B5035, then continue straight where it bends sharply left. Turn left onto the B5036 and head back to Black Rock.

That's this ride done, but there are plenty of others suited to retro bike-riding in this part of the country. The Monsal Trail, as well as parts of the Limestone Way and Midshires Way, work for this kind of bike, and there is a joy in preserving or bringing back to life a retro steel race bike, or one of the early mountain bikes. A growing number of festivals and retro rides also celebrate this part of cycling. Rex Coley would have loved to see that.

12 HARDCORE 100
A challenging route in the Derbyshire Peak District

WILDNESS RATING **6/10** HARDNESS RATING **8/10**

This route was designed by Paul Gregory, who runs a series of challenge events through his business Velotastic. They all fit into the ethos of *Really Wild Cycling*. 'My events are what I call a big day out on the bike,' Paul told me when he gave me his permission to include this one, 'but I also make them achievable. I remember one participant in particular describing a route I'd designed as "A ba*tard of a route, but you can do it." That pleased me, because it's exactly what I aim for in every ride I organise.'

Hardcore 100 uses back lanes and bridleways that only an experienced cyclist like Paul Gregory, who has lived and cycled on the edge of the Peak District for thirty years, would know. He has a natural eye, like so many experienced cyclists, for the way less travelled, and he enjoys letting his instincts take him where they will.

Hardcore 100 is a joy to ride, and its challenge lies in in the total of 2,100 metres of elevation gain in 100 kilometres, meaning there is hardly any flat riding at all.

As a circular ride Hardcore 100 can be started anywhere on its route, but the villages just west of Chesterfield are ideal because Chesterfield is a transport hub. Also, going out west and coming back east is often the best way in the UK to ensure a tailwind for the second half of any bike ride.

So, from our start in Holmesfield, once home to the Labour Party politician and activist for walkers' rights Bert Ward, head west along Main Street to Horsleygate Lane, where you turn left. Look for Grimsell Lane on your left, which is the first section of roughish track. Follow Grimsell Lane south to Millthorpe, where you go right on the B6051 to

FACT FILE

Where The Derbyshire Dales	**Ride Distance** 100 kilometres (62 miles)
Start and finish Holmesfield	**Highest point** Taddington Moor, 421 metres
OS reference SK 326 779	(1,381 feet)

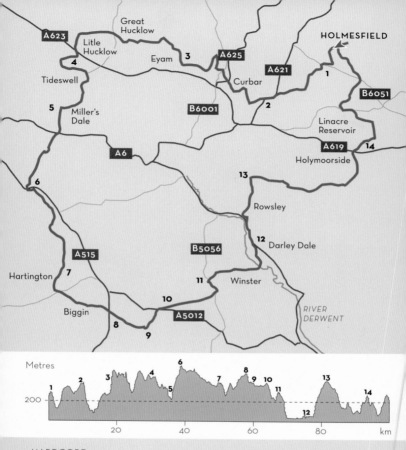

HARDCORE 100
Track Elevation

MAP KEY

1 Left through Unthank to the A621
2 Start of trail diversion to Wellington's Monument then back to road and descend to Curbar
3 Very steep climb to Eyam Edge
4 Bridleway to Weston
5 Start of Priestcliffe Road
6 Pick up High Peak Trail after crossing A515 and go south-east
7 Right fork to Hartington
8 Left off A515 onto Cardlemere Lane
9 Left onto Parwich Lane then right on Mouldridge Lane to A5012
10 Go straight to Winster
11 Turn right into Clough Lane to Darley Bridge, rough surface in places
12 Pick up the Peak Heritage Railway and go north
13 Right into Beeley Bar Lane
14 Start of bridleway through Ducksick and Linacre woods

Unthank Lane. Here you turn left and head for the village of Unthank.

There are several places called Unthank in the UK, and according to the *Oxford Dictionary of British Place Names* it doesn't mean the inhabitants of those places were at some time lacking in gratitude. The name Unthank is thought to derive from the seventh-century English word 'unpance', which means without leave. So the various Unthanks around the country mark areas of land that were originally occupied unlawfully.

Unthank Lane goes right through the village and out the other side, where there's a long uphill section that goes through Burrs Wood to the junction with Far Lane. Turn right here. You are now on top of an open plateau. Go right, then left on Fox Lane, then left again to ride a short stretch of the A621, before going right at the first crossroads onto Clodhall Lane.

Stay on Clodhall Lane for 200 metres, then go left onto a bridleway called Bar Road. This takes you south-west past Wellington's

Monument, then north along Baslow Edge, a rock formation typical of this area, where the gritstone of the northern and eastern Peak District meets the largely limestone scenery of the central and south side.

The views are incredible all along this off-road section, which takes you back to Clodhall Lane, where you go left and descend to Curbar. Turn right in the centre of Curbar and follow the signs to Froggatt, where you go left over the River Derwent to the junction with the B6001. Go right on the B6001, then left on the B6521 and head for Eyam, where in 1666 the brave residents agreed to quarantine themselves to prevent the spread of an outbreak of plague. Only 83 from Eyam's then population of 350 survived while the disease ran its course, but the villagers' decision contained something that could have decimated the population of the whole area.

Continue west past Eyam Church, then turn right up Hawkhill Road for the start of one of the Hardcore 100's steepest climbs. The road rises at an average of 14% for 800 metres up Eyam Edge. Turn left at the top, ride along Eyam Edge, then away from it before turning left onto Sir William Hill Road. After 100 metres go right on an uneven track and follow the track to Bretton. Turn right in Bretton, then fork right where the road splits, heading towards Great Hucklow Wood. Turn left on the bridleway going through the wood, then descend to Great Hucklow village.

Turn right at the T-junction in the village, then fork right at a small triangular green and follow a narrow lane that becomes a bridleway. Cross the B6049 to another surfaced lane and follow this into Little Hucklow. Go right, then left, at the last houses in Little Hucklow, then take the first left, crossing the A623, towards Tideswell. Once over the main road look for a bridleway on your left and follow it to Wheston. Turn left in Wheston and ride east to the centre of Tideswell, where you go right along Queen Street to Town End, and then turn right on Richard Lane, then left onto Meadow Lane.

Meadow Lane leads to Miller's Dale, where you go right and follow the B6049 for a kilometre. Cross the River Wye on this road and, just where a long, left bend of the B6049 starts, there's a stony track on your left: turn left and follow this track uphill to Priestcliffe Road, where you go right to the A6. Carefully cross the A6 and head south-west on Sough Lane, which is

also the Limestone Way long-distance trail. Turn right on Moor Lane and continue south-west to the A515.

Turn right at the main road to pick up the start of the High Peak Trail, and follow it south-east to the surfaced road crossing at Parsley Hay car park. Turn right on the road, then left at the T-junction, then take the right fork, where this lane splits, to Hartington, which is about 800 metres from the

Staffordshire border. Cross the B5054 and ride up Hall Bank, past Hartington Hall Youth Hostel, and go right on Highfield Lane.

This leads to the top of Biggin Dale, one of the many valleys that give rise to the name, Derbyshire Dales. Continue to a junction where four lanes meet. Cross the junction and follow Main Street through Biggin. Turn right on the A515 Buxton Road, then immediately left onto Cardlemere Lane. Follow Cardlemere Lane, which becomes Cobblersnook Lane, to its junction with Parwich Lane. Turn left on Parwich Lane, then right on Mouldridge Lane to the A5012, where you turn right.

Follow the A5012 for 700 metres until it bends right. Here you follow the lane that continues straight over the crossroads towards Winster. Go left on the B5056 before reaching the village,

then almost immediate right, and follow West Bank to Main Street, which is the B5057. Turn left here and follow Elton Road past Winster Cemetery before turning right onto Birchover Lane, which is another tough climb in a day full of tough climbs.

At the top of the hill in Upper Town, and just past Birchover Wood, turn right onto Clough Lane. This quickly becomes a rough track and heads downhill through a wooded area to Darley Bridge. Take care on this section, because some bits are steep and the surface is bad. Turn left onto the B5057 and head towards Darley Dale, a village more often referred to locally as Darley, but go left before you reach there on Church Road.

After 800 metres you reach the Peak Rail heritage railway. Turn left and follow the cycle path to Rowsley. Leave the path of the railway at the car park on Old Station Close and go right on the A6 for 100 metres, before turning left onto the B6012, Chatsworth Road. Follow this road north until the sharp left bend that takes it over the River Derwent, where you go right onto Beeley Bar Lane, and the start of another long uphill slog.

You eventually reach the top at a car park on Beeley Lane. Turn left and ride across Beeley Moor, going left on Harland Lane to cross Longside Road and join Harewood Road, which you follow all the way to Holymoorside. On entering the village turn left on

Gallery Lane, cross Lords Road and continue in a northerly direction up Chandler Hill Lane to a main road. Turn right onto the main road, then go almost immediately left at Ladywood Garage.

This road, Westwick Lane, becomes bridleway after Westwick Farm. Follow it to Ashgate Road, turn left there, and in 100 metres look for a bridleway on your right. Go right and follow the bridleway through Ducksick Wood to Linacre Wood, where the surface improves near Linacre Lower Reservoir. Continue to the B6050, where you turn left, then go right in Overgreen on Grange Lane.

Follow Grange Lane down to Oxton Rakes, then up to Bolehill, where you go left to Commonside. Turn left on the B6051 Valley Road, then go right on the eastern edge of Commonside. Turn left at the T-junction onto Highlightly Lane, looking for a bridleway on almost your immediate right. This bridleway takes you all the way back to Holmesfield to complete this version of the Hardcore 100.

It's a great route and a tribute to its creator, Paul Gregory, but it's typical of the kind many cyclists create for themselves. Paul updates it most years before the challenge event, so even if you ride this version you'll find something new if you take part in his official Hardcore 100 event. Check out his website, www.velotastic.co.uk, for details.

13 SPINAL TAP
A ride along the spine of the Lincolnshire Wolds

WILDNESS RATING **5/10** HARDNESS RATING **5/10**

Riding along the apex, or spine, of a range of hills, using minor roads and/or trails, is an enjoyable cycling challenge both in the planning and the execution. I chose the Lincolnshire Wolds for this book because navigation is fairly simple there, but upland areas almost anywhere will do, especially if surrounded by flat terrain.

Many years ago, before it was drained to create arable farmland, much of low-lying Lincolnshire was wet and often flooded, so the best way to travel up and down the county in those days was to follow the ridge of the Wolds. The same happened in other parts of the country, giving rise to ancient transport links called ridgeways.

Once the flatlands of Lincolnshire were drained transport was made much easier, so the north–south main roads are all on the flat now, with other main roads cutting through the Wolds from east to west to link them. This resulted in the old ways along the top of the Wolds becoming quiet back roads, and this ride uses them to travel the length of the Lincolnshire Wolds, from their southern tip to their northern extremity.

Planning your own route over the long axis of a range of hills, as opposed to following a marked trail like the Pennine Bridleway (a good thing to do in itself, so I've included it in the book), is fun. The Yorkshire Wolds, for example, lend themselves to this, if you use bits of the Wolds Way and replace the footpath sections with minor roads (again, I've done this in this book).

I went south to north along the Lincolnshire Wolds, so Old Bolingbroke to Barton-upon-Humber,

FACT FILE

Where Lincolnshire	**OS reference** TA 032 225
Start Old Bolingbroke	**Ride distance** 81 kilometres (50½ miles)
OS reference TF 349 651	**Highest point** Whitegate Hill, Caistor, 142 metres (466 feet)
Finish Barton-upon-Humber	

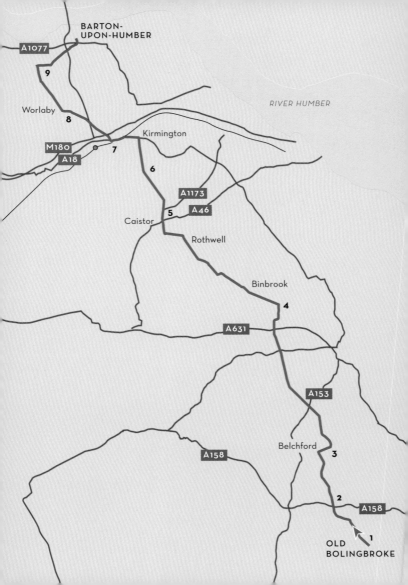

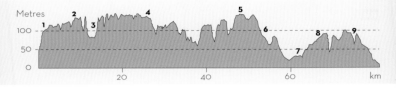

MAP KEY

1 Horncastle Hill
2 Take care crossing the A158
3 Go right in Belchford and climb Belchford Hill. Left at summit
4 Veer left and ride down Limber Hill to Binbrook
5 Continue north where A1173 goes sharp right
6 Go left where minor road forks
7 Go right off A18 at Melton Ross, then first left to climb
8 Cross the B1206 then go right before Worlaby
9 Turn right just before electricity pylons

at the southern and northern feet of the hills respectively. They can be linked by a fairly direct route across the Wolds' tops, which is the challenge of doing this ridge line exercise.

Once on the tops the ride sticks around the 130- to 140-metre contours, with a few dips down into river valleys where the porous surface stratum – chalk, limestone or sandstone here – is worn down to the impermeable mudstone and clay layer that underlies the Lincolnshire Wolds.

Old Bolingbroke is old by name and nature. The castle site is a grassy mound today, but the first castle was built on it during the twelfth century. It was replaced in the thirteenth century, and was the birthplace of King Henry IV. The castle was badly damaged in 1643, when it was a Royalist garrison and under siege from the Roundheads.

After that it fell into a steady state of disrepair, finally toppling over completely in 1815, when most of the site was cleared.

Start outside the church towards the northern edge of the village and head east. Take the first right and ride up Horncastle Hill, which is quite steep at first. This takes you up to the gently rounded top of the Wolds. Look behind you from here and on a clear day you can see Boston Stump, the 81.3-metre-high (266 feet) tower of St Botolph's, Boston's impressive parish church.

Old Bolingbroke is old by name and nature. The castle site is a grassy mound today, but the first castle was built on it during the twelfth century.

Continue north-west to the B1195. Turn left, ride through Winceby and past the site of the Civil War Battle of Winceby, then go left onto the A158 and take the first right after 200 metres. Continue north through Greetham. You are on top of the Wolds now, following the flat ridge line of the hills, with fantastic views on either side.

There's a little dip down into a

Caistor is an interesting place if you want to drop down for a visit. It was founded as a Roman camp and has several interesting old buildings, including Caistor Grammar School.

valley at Belchford, where you go right in the centre of the village to climb Belchford Hill and back to the top of the Wolds. Go left at the summit to join the Bluestone Heath Road, the original ridgeway along the Lincolnshire Wolds, which was an old drovers' way along the top of the hills.

Keep on this road, trending north-west, crossing several other roads, until you descend Limber Hill into Binbrook. Turn left on the B1203, then go straight on to join a minor road going north-west where the B1203 goes sharp left. Continue uphill past Binbrook Airfield, formerly RAF Binbrook and a Bomber Command base during the Second World War. Keep riding in a north-westerly

direction; there's another dip down into and out of the village of Thoresway, and another at Rothwell. From Rothwell centre follow the road signposted to Caistor. Turn right on the B1225, and briefly join the A1173 heading north so you can stay on the ridge line. Caistor is an interesting place if you want to drop down for a visit. It was founded as a Roman camp and has several interesting old buildings, including Caistor Grammar School, which dates back to 1633.

If you remain on the ridge, then continue north where the A1173 turns sharp right, then go left where the minor road forks to begin your descent from the Wolds ridge to the flatlands. You pass Humberside International Airport on your way to Kirmington, one of the lowest points in the Lincolnshire Wolds.

The gap it's in, through which the A18 runs, was caused by erosion by ice during the Ice Age, and to cross it you have to turn left and ride along the A18 for 3 kilometres to Melton Ross, where you turn right, then take the first left to climb back up to the Wolds ridge top, after riding past Elsham to the top of Elsham Hill.

Turn right just before entering Worlaby to ride along the edge of the very steep north-west scarp of the Wolds. Turn right after 5.5 kilometres, just before two sets of electricity lines, and descend to Barton-upon-Humber and journey's end.

14 SAMPLING SARN HELEN

One of the wilder sections of a much longer ancient Roman way

WILDNESS RATING 8/10 HARDNESS RATING 8/10

Sarn Helen is the collective name for a network of roads that served as the central nervous system for transport and trade when Wales was occupied by Rome. The roads formed a north–south link, with the first leg from Aberconwy to Brecon, where it split in two. A second leg headed from there to Neath in South Wales, while a third went to Carmarthen in the south-west of the country.

Much of what formed the main route of Sarn Helen is now bridleway or less-travelled minor road, so it's a perfect route for adventurous cyclists. In 1998 Mountain Bike Routes UK (MBRUK) published details of their Sarn Helen Trail, a 270-mile epic adventure ride from Llandudno on the north coast to Worms Head in the south. For more information on the Sarn Helen Trail, which is a multi-day

bike-packing challenge, and how to ride it, including the opportunity to buy MBRUK's excellent guidebooks, see www.mbruk.co.uk.

This ride follows alternating minor roads and bridleways, various stretches of which were part of Sarn Helen in Roman times. It takes in the start of the Carmarthen leg, coming out of Brecon, and is an example of what Sarn Helen has to offer, although there are much tougher sections than this on the whole Trail. And, like the whole Sarn Helen Trail, the Sample is more suited to riding on a mountain bike than any other kind.

The ride starts and finishes in Brecon, at the southern end of what was once the Kingdom of Powys. There's a roundabout where the A40 is joined by the A470 and the road into Brecon through Llanfaes. Riding away from Brecon on the Llanfaes road, take the third exit from the roundabout and

FACT FILE

Where The Brecon Beacons in Wales

Start and finish Just south of Brecon, Powys

OS reference SO 032 284

Ride distance 47.5 kilometres (29¾ miles)

Highest point Bryn Melyn, 473 metres (1,551 feet)

follow this quiet road uphill. Take the left branch where the road forks after Tyisha, then continue for another 500 metres. By this point the land either side of the road has changed from fields to more scrubby land.

A bridleway crosses the road at an angle of 45 degrees. Go left on this bridleway and follow it over a flat shelf of land. It's a bit rough and rutted in places. After a surfaced section, which is the drive to a house, the bridleway crosses another minor road at a bend in it.

Continue across the road, heading south-westerly along the bridleway, which again has several deep ruts carved out by tractor tyres. You are better off riding between the ruts on the raised area of scrubby grass,

because some are so deep you will catch your pedals in them.

After passing some farm buildings on your left you come to the A4215. Cross the main road with care and go straight ahead on a minor road that becomes a bridleway at Forest Lodge. Follow the bridleway, which is rough in places, so take care.

You climb steadily now around the flanks of the steep-sided Fan Frynych. Its 629-metre summit is typical of the Brecon Beacons, a flat peak with steep craggy sides sculpted millions of years ago by the ice that covered this region during the last Ice Age.

A short descent leads into Nant Cwm-du, and you cross the bridge there. Once over the bridge, if you look up to your left there are some

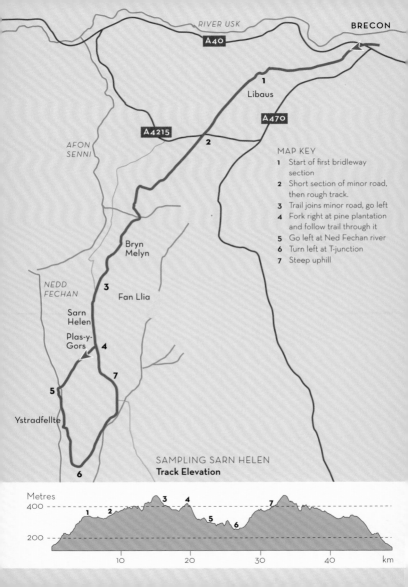

RIVER USK

BRECON

A40

1
Libaus

A470

A4215

AFON
SENNI

2

MAP KEY

1 Start of first bridleway
   section
2 Short section of minor road,
   then rough track.
3 Trail joins minor road, go left
4 Fork right at pine plantation
   and follow trail through it
5 Go left at Ned Fechan river
6 Turn left at T-junction
7 Steep uphill

Bryn
Melyn

3

NEDD
FECHAN

Fan Llia

Sarn
Helen

Plas-y-
Gors   4

7

5

Ystradfellte

6

SAMPLING SARN HELEN
Track Elevation

Metres
400

200

1   2   3   4   5   6   7

10   20   30   40   km

impressive crags: they're called Craig Cwm-du. Take a minute for a deep breath, because there's a long, tough climb up ahead.

This takes you almost across a shoulder of Fan Frynych called Bryn Melyn, the highest point of this ride. The trail surface is a bit rough going up, but the summit view west across the valley carved by the infant Afon Senni is incredible. Behind you is the bulk of another mountain, Fan Llia, where another river is born, Afon Llia, which flows off in the opposite direction to the Senni.

Descending from Bryn Melyn watch out for the stream crossings, which can all be forded unless the weather has been very wet, so pick a

dry window for doing this ride and always take care when riding through water. The trail eventually joins a minor road: turn left onto this road and follow it south alongside the Llia.

After 1.5 kilometres on the road you reach a small pine plantation called Plas-y-Gors. Turn right off the road and follow the trail through the trees in a south-westerly direction. It climbs dead straight for a kilometre, and then you descend quite steeply to the Nedd Fechan river, also known as the Little Neath. It eventually becomes simply the River Neath and flows into the Bristol Channel in Swansea Bay.

Turn right onto a surfaced road at Blaennedd Farm, and follow this rolling but downhill-inclining road to a

T-junction, where you go left. Now you are riding up the River Mellte valley and back on the path of the old Sarn Helen road, but heading north back towards Brecon.

After 2 kilometres you reach the tiny village of Ystradfellte, a lovely place that is very popular with hill walkers, canoeists and cavers. Just before the village you pass close to Porth-yr-Ogof, a cave into which the River Mellte flows.

Porth-yr-Ogof has the biggest cave entrance in Wales, but it's a place for cave experts only. There have been eleven deaths in it since 1957. The word Mellte means lightning, and the river gets its name because in wet weather it rises very quickly, flows very rapidly, and is extremely cold. All but one of Porth-yr-Ogof's death toll were caught out and swept away by the rapid-flowing Mellte.

Further up the valley, where the Llia joins the Mellte, the road rears up ahead of you. Climb for about a kilometre, then after another flat kilometre you are back in the Plas-y-Gors plantation. From there you retrace your outward journey back to Brecon.

The Sarn Helen Trail has lots to offer anyone looking for an off-the-beaten-track adventure. Sections of it can be done as day rides, or you can follow the full MBRUK route, which is non-stop mountains and has a total height gain greater than Everest.

15 ON THE BEACHES
A hilly coastal adventure
in wild Wales

WILDNESS RATING **5/10** HARDNESS RATING **7/10**

How many beaches can you visit on one bike ride? It's a great game to play on any stretch of coast, but peninsulas lend themselves to beach-bagging. 'On the Beaches' is a ride around the northernmost of Pembrokeshire's peninsulas visiting ten exquisite, quiet and clean beaches in 64 kilometres of road cycling, with the option of a few more beaches if you don't mind a bit of walking with your bike. Plus there's the bonus of riding through little-changed Pembrokeshire back-country, which for road conditions and landscape is like riding through the 1950s.

On the Beaches is a ride to do for its own sake, but like others in the book it's also a template that can be applied to anywhere in the world. Much of the UK coastline lends itself to rides like this: circular routes linking beaches and headlands. Doing them on peninsulas works best because of their high coastline-to-interior ratio. Pembrokeshire has other peninsulas, and there are more in the rest of Wales. East Kent and parts of the Yorkshire coast lend themselves to rides like this. So do the Isle of Purbeck, north Norfolk and the Furness peninsula. Scotland offers many much wilder examples, some of them real cycling adventures. And almost any island is good for beach-bagging.

Then there's Cornwall, where the further west you are almost every bike ride of even medium length passes a beach. I've chosen Pembrokeshire because in many respects it is Cornwall without the crowds. The county is a less well-known tourist destination, and for cyclists that makes it all the better. Pembrokeshire has a similar coastline to Cornwall

---

FACT FILE

Where Pembrokeshire	**Ride distance** 64 kilometres (40 miles)
Start and finish St David's	**Highest point** Mathry, 130 metres (426 feet)
OS reference SM 752 252	

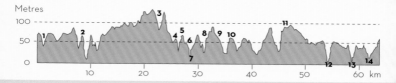

Metres

100 -

50 -

0

10   20   30   40   50   60   km

ON THE BEACHES
Track Elevation

1   Caerfi Bay
2   Turn right in Middle Hill
    and ride to Solva Beach
    and back
3   Steep descent, take care
4   Turn left at crossroads and
    descend to Aber Mawr
5   Go right after visiting Aber
    Mawr Beach
6   Go right to Abercastle
7   Continue through Trefin to
    beach at Aber Draw

8   Aber Draw
9   Go right to Porth Gain
     and back
10   First right to Abereiddy
     and Abereiddy Bay
11   Turn right to
     Whitesands Bay
12   Whitesands Bay
13   St Justinian
14   Porth Clais

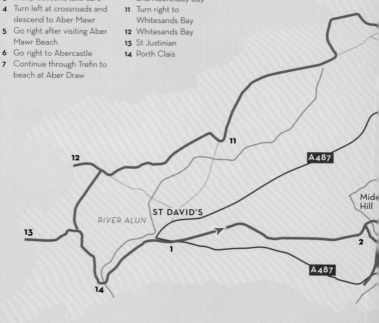

with masses of unspoilt and spectacular beaches, all of them clean and far less crowded. The interior of Pembrokeshire is more attractive than Cornwall's, too, and its roads are much quieter. Altogether, Pembrokeshire is a hidden gem of a county, especially for cyclists, and well worth getting to know.

This ride takes in both sides, as well as the tip, of a west-facing peninsula – it's beach-bagging at its best. The ride starts and finishes in St David's, a small town whose cathedral makes it officially a city, the resting place of David, the patron saint of Wales. With a population of 1,841 as of 2011, St David's is the smallest city in Great Britain.

St David touches almost every part of the city named after him. He was born around AD 500 just south of St David's, next to the sea in St Non's Bay, which is named after his mother. David founded a monastery on the banks of the River Alun, near to where the cathedral is now, and was made a saint because of the care he and his monks gave the sick, poor and needy.

Start on High Street, in sight of St David's Cathedral, and head east to join the A487 for about 100 metres until the first crossroads, where you go right on Ffordd Caerfei. After a kilometre(ish) you reach Caerfei Bay. You can see the beach from the road end, but if you want to do this exercise properly and

stand on it, you must walk a hundred metres or so with your bike to do so.

When that's done, mount up: there are nine more beaches to go. Ride back to the A487 crossroads and go right onto the main road. After 300 metres go left at a school onto a minor road. This goes straight for another kilometre to a junction; turn right and follow a road called the Ffos y Mynach. Follow this around a small airfield, after which the road dips steeply into the Solva river valley to Middle Mill.

Turn right just before the bridge onto a road called Prendergast, and head south. This takes you to Main Street, the A487, in Solva. Go right on Main Street and you quickly reach beach two, which is on the Solva estuary. It's mainly a harbour, but there is a beach at low tide and a more permanent strip of sand on the other side of a footbridge. There are plenty of cafés, too. Solva is a really nice place with lots going on, but when you've seen enough ride back to Middle Mill.

Turn right at the T-junction in Middle Mill, take the second left and climb out of the Solva valley. Go straight at the first crossroads and left at the second. You will come to a T-junction: turn right. Keep left at the first road fork, and right at the second. Go left at the next crossroads to Treffynnon, right at the T-junction in the village, then first right along a tree-lined road. Cross the B4330 and head for Mathry.

Mathry is an unspoilt Pembroke-shire village that sits on top of a conical hill, and has been there since the 1500s and the reign of Edward III. You have to cross the A487 (with care) to enter the village, but a brief glimpse of what living in rural peace is like, so long as the main road isn't too busy, makes visiting the village well worth it.

Turn right just before the church and descend Mathry Hill. It's quite steep, and the village road ends back at the A487, so take extra care. Turn left just before the main road onto a minor one, then ride 3 kilometres to a crossroads, where you go left. A steep descent then takes you to a T-junction: turn left and continue gently downhill to Aber Mawr and beach number three.

It's a mostly shingle beach with bad sea currents. Ships have been wrecked here, with bodies washed up all along this beach. The beach was also the site of one of the first inter-country telegraph cable links, laid in 1862 and linking the UK with Ireland through Wexford. A short walk north along the Pembrokeshire Coast Path and you can clock up an extra beach, a tiny one called Aber Bach.

Back on the bike, retrace the way you got to Aber Mawr until you pass the head of a small wooded valley shortly after Woodlands Farm. Take the first right, still in the trees, and follow this road through Morfa, going right to Abercastle and beach number four.

Retrace to the single road junction in Abercastle, and go right to Trefin.

Ride through the village, then a kilometre west of it is beach five, Aber Draw. You have to walk your bike a short distance along the coast path to stand on it, though.

When you are back on your bike continue west to Llanrhian, where you go right at the crossroads and descend to sea level at beach six, Porthgain. There's only really a beach here at low tide, but the harbour is interesting. The giant hoppers on the harbour wall are relics of an industrial past. Porthgain harbour was built to ship out slate from local quarries, and when the slate trade ended hoppers were built to contain crushed dolerite used to surface roads.

Return to Llanrhian and go right at the crossroads. Take the first right to Abereiddy and Abereiddy Bay, beach seven. They come thick and fast now, so back on your bike, go right and up a steep hill and right again at the T-junction. Keep going for another couple of kilometres, then start looking for signs on your right to Whitesands and the B4583. Beach number eight lies a kilometre down this road, and it's the biggest and busiest of the ride, a destination for families, surfers and all who enjoy beach life.

Whitesands is also popular with archaeologists, historians and pilgrims, with St David having been educated here in a house that overlooked the beach, while St Patrick is said to have sailed from here in AD 432 to convert Ireland to

Christianity. To the north of Whitesands Bay St David's Head curls around two very secluded beaches; both are within easy walking distance.

Two more beaches to go. Saddle up and retrace along the B4583, taking the first right turn after the golf course. Follow this road past a farm called Treleddyn to a T-junction. Turn right,

and after a kilometre you should reach the lifeboat station at St Justinian. There's just a tiny bit of rocky beach here at low tide, but it's a spectacular bit of coastline nevertheless. Look south from here and you can see Pen Dal-aderyn, the westernmost tip of mainland Wales, and off it Ramsey Island.

Retrace and go right at the T-junction, right again and keep straight to the tiny rocky beach of Port Clais at the mouth of the River Alun. Continue north-west up a steep hill and follow this road, which runs along the edge of Merry Vale, back to St David's to end the ride near St David's Cathedral.

16 HEAVEN AND HELL
Three hard climbs,
with lovely lakes in between

WILDNESS RATING **7/10** HARDNESS RATING **8/10**

This is a road ride, but it's on lonely roads that are far from anywhere. It's a challenge, too, one that kicks off with one of the toughest climbs in the UK, then descends to a fairy-tale lake before another high climb, another lake, and a final up and helter-skelter down. The ride is 72.5 kilometres (45 miles) long, but it's a tough 45 miles, a front-loaded climbing challenge with the first hill one of the hardest most people will ever encounter.

You start in the Tolkienesque village of Dinas Mawddwy, which is on the A470 about 10 miles west of Dolgellau at the southern edge of Snowdonia. Head north-east on the minor road and keep right to follow the Afon Dyfi stream. You are surrounded by mountains, with the higher Aran range peaking at 907 metres on your left. There are 9 kilometres of easy riding along the valley bottom, steadily gaining height but nothing major, then the road swings right and you are at the bottom of Hell.

It was called Hellfire Pass by English motor manufacturers, who used the unrelenting incline in front of you to test their cars. The hill is called Bwlch y Groes in Welsh, and in any language it's steep, a real contender for UK cycling's hardest hill. The Bwlch rises to 545 metres, making it the highest surfaced pass in Wales. Officially it gains 385 metres in 3.6 kilometres, giving an average gradient of just under 11%, but its crux is the final 1.78 kilometres, that start out at 25% and get steeper the higher you go. There's nowhere to hide, no lessening of gradient. It's a long slog to the top, but the view is worth it, if you pick a clear day. And you have the descent into a heavenly landscape to come.

FACT FILE

Where Southern Snowdonia, North Wales	**Ride distance** 72.5 kilometres (45 miles)
Start and finish Dinas Mawddwy	**Highest point** Summit of Bwlch y Groes, 545 metres (1,788 feet)
OS reference SH 188 693	

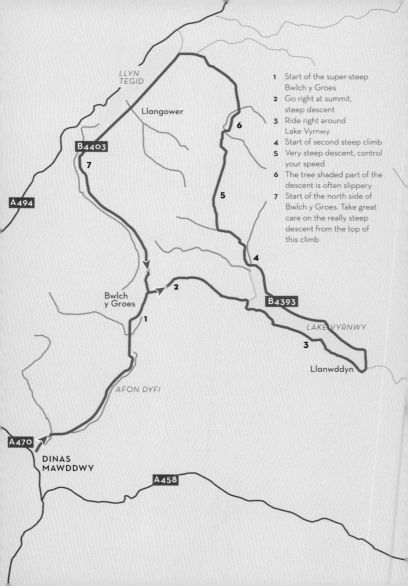

LLYN
TEGID

Llangower

B4403

7

A494

1 Start of the super-steep
  Bwlch y Groes
2 Go right at summit,
  steep descent
3 Ride right around
  Lake Vyrnwy
4 Start of second steep climb
5 Very steep descent, control
  your speed
6 The tree shaded part of the
  descent is often slippery
7 Start of the north side of
  Bwlch y Groes. Take great
  care on the really steep
  descent from the top of
  this climb

6

5

4

2

Bwlch
y Groes

1

B4393

3

LAKE VYRNWY

Llanwddyn

AFON DYFI

A470

DINAS
MAWDDWY

A458

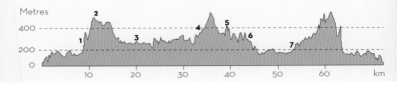

HEAVEN AND HELL
Track Elevation

There's something unreal about Lake Vyrnwy. Take the first right turn near the top of Bwlch y Groes and descend to the lake, which looks enchanted. It's surrounded by tightly packed conifer trees, a dark mysterious plantation concealing a velvety floor of mossy boulders. A Gothic tower emerges from the water, looking like a fairy-tale castle, but its purpose is more mundane. Lake Vyrnwy is a reservoir built for the people of Liverpool, and the Gothic tower was built to beautify the equipment used to process the water taken from it.

It's still a gorgeous place, though. Turn right at the bottom of the descent and ride around the lake, crossing the dam wall – a great place to stop and look down into the Vyrnwy valley, especially when water is let out through high-up outlets to feed the River Vyrnwy. It crashes down the dam wall below you and looks, and sounds, spectacular.

Turn left at the end of the dam wall and follow the road around the lake until the car park at its northernmost

tip, where two small rivers join, then flow into it. This is the start of the next long climb, which after a steep start will be much gentler on your legs than the Bwlch was.

After topping out at 502 metres you descend, steeply at first but gentler later on. There are several bends, so take care. Take care too when you pass through the steep-sided Penllyn Forest section of the descent, which is overhung by trees, so the road here stays wet, and can be slippery for much longer than the rest of the descent. Finally, watch out for the final bit of the descent, which drops steeply just before joining a main road.

Turn left onto the main road, then go left again onto the B4403 at the north-eastern end of Lake Bala. This was the largest natural body of water in Wales anyway, but was made bigger when the engineer Thomas Telford raised its water level to help feed one of his canals. The River Dee runs through Lake Bala, which is called Tegid in Welsh, a word that conveys fairness or beauty. It certainly is a beautiful lake.

Next comes a nice flat 7-kilometre ride along the lake shore, next to the Bala Lake narrow-gauge railway on which steam engines haul sightseers from Bala station to Llanuwchllyn. That's where you leave Lake Bala, going left to start the final climb. This is the other side of Bwlch y Groes, which, although it takes you to the pass summit, is nowhere near as steep as the side you've already climbed.

The summit is a good place to stop and consider Bwlch y Groes in all its glory. And to consider the competitors in the Tour of Britain and Milk Race, the UK's biggest cycling stage race at the time, during the 1950s, 1960s and 1970s. The race organisers loved sending the riders up the steep side of Bwlch y Groes, but in those days the smallest chainrings available to them had forty-two teeth, maybe thirty-nine teeth later in the 1970s. With a maximum sprocket size of twenty-four or twenty-six teeth, even some of the best and strongest of their generation had to walk parts of the Bwlch pushing their bikes.

Now, take care on the descent: not only is the road steep, but it's also bumpy in places. Keep your speed down to well within your comfort zone, and slow to crawling pace for the final left bend, the one where you turned right to hit the start of the hardest section. All that's left now is a gently downhill ride back to Dinas Mawddwy to complete this heavenly challenge with a bit of Hell thrown in.

17 WILD ROAD TO WORLD'S END
An off-the-beaten-track road ride
just inside North Wales

WILDNESS RATING **6/10** HARDNESS RATING **6/10**

The UK has plenty of wild roads as well as off-road trails, and this ride is all on surfaced roads, although most are single-track and some are as bumpy as bridleways can be. The road to World's End is wild due to its isolation, the scenery around it and because it isn't in a popular tourist location.

That's the challenge, delight and reward of a ride like this: looking for wild places where you might not expect them. You don't have to go to the far north of Scotland or to the wildest parts of our National Parks: this ride starts 4 kilometres outside Wrexham, and Liverpool is less than 40 kilometres away. There's really wild cycling in all sorts of places, if you look for it.

The ride is a circuit around a range of three rounded mountain tops: Eglwyseg, Ruabon and Esclusham,

right at the north-eastern edge of Wales. Route-finding in the first half of the ride looks complicated because there are many twists and turns, but it's actually quite easy: you always stick to the road highest up the mountain sides.

The target of the ride is a place called World's End: an extraordinary place, as you'll see when you get there. It got its name from the days when the road you'll follow was a packhorse trail; the valley sides are so steep and there was so little trace of human habitation that people using it christened the head of a valley where a tributary of the River Dee is born, World's End.

It's an enchanting place, though, hidden by pine trees and dead quiet but for birdsong and the gurgle of flowing water, but best visited in the summer months. There are a few very isolated dwellings around World's End,

FACT FILE

Where Wrexham County Borough, north-east Wales	**Ride distance** 32 kilometres (20 miles)
Start and finish Minera	**Highest point** Summit after World's End, 421 metres (1,381 feet)
OS reference SJ 271 518	

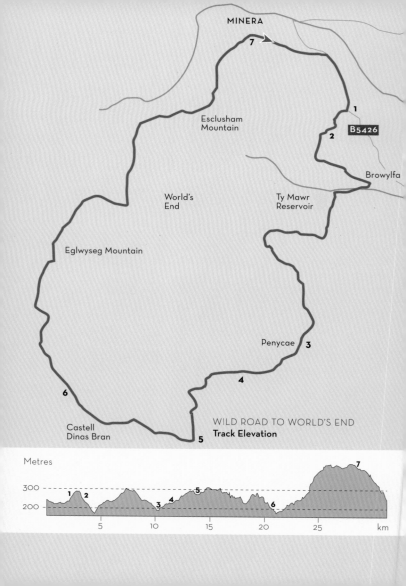

MINERA

7

1

B5426

2

Browylfa

Esclusham
Mountain

World's
End

Ty Mawr
Reservoir

Eglwyseg Mountain

Penycae

3

4

6

5

Castell
Dinas Bran

WILD ROAD TO WORLD'S END
Track Elevation

Metres

300

200

1 2   3 4   5   6   7

5   10   15   20   25   km

MAP KEY

1 Turn right off B5426 at
   Hafon Wen
2 Keep right, then follow
   the road south then east
   Browylfa
3 Turn sharp right on entering
   Penycae

4 Follow this road until at
   T-junction
5 Go right at T-junction
6 Follow the single track road
   around the mountain
7 Turn left and descend to
   Minera

and as recently as 2014 they were cut off for six weeks by snow.

I started the ride in Minera because it's near to Wrexham, which has good transport links with the rest of the country. Minera, as you might have guessed, got its name from mining; lead and zinc ores in particular. That ended here in the early 1900s, but the buildings above the Meadow Shaft of the Minera Lead Mines have been preserved, and you ride past them soon after leaving the village.

Cross the River Clywedog that flows along the southern edge of Minera, climb a short hill and turn left at the top to start the mountain circuit. Turn right off B5426 at Hafon Wen. Continue past the road end to Mutton Hall. This road then bends sharp left: follow it left to Bronwylfa, where you go very sharp right towards Ty Mawr Reservoir.

The Road to World's End can be done on a road bike, although you'll need robust tyres on it, but if you are riding a bike with off-road capability, like a cyclo-cross or a gravel bike, there's an extra loop you can do here around the reservoir. Otherwise

stay on the road and follow it to Onan Fawr Farm.

Go right at the farm and follow this road up and down the mountainside to Penycae. Turn sharp right on entering the village. Follow this road to a T-junction above a very steep-sided valley. Go right and around the bottom of the mountain circuit. Direction-finding is much simpler now as there is only one road to follow, and it takes you all the way back to Minera.

You can bask in the peace and quiet on this bit. Few mechanised road users come up here – grass growing along the

centre of the road is testament to that – although it has always been popular with adventurous local cyclists. The road undulates below a series of wild high crags as you slowly change direction from riding south to riding north. Llangollen lies in the valley below, although your view over it is slightly obstructed by a hill with the remains of a castle, Castell Dinas Bran, on top. It was built there for Gruffydd Maelor II, a Prince of Powys Fadog, in the 1260s.

What you do get is a clear view of the River Dee and the Shropshire Union Canal; both go through Llangollen. The Dee Valley runs west-to-east here, so as you progress further north you leave it

behind to ride up the side valley of one of its tributaries, the Eglwyseg, which flows from Eglwyseg Mountain. This valley is the crux of the ride, the hardest and longest uphill section; the climb to World's End.

The riding up the Eglwyseg Valley is a wonderful experience: the climb is committing, but the views and solitude do plenty to ameliorate the pain. For most of the way you ride against the flow of the Eglwyseg, which babbles and rushes beside you. Then, where the road enters an area concealed by pine trees and flexes sharply left like a giant elbow, the Eglwyseg flows across the road right at the apex of the bend. This is World's End.

The ford requires respect if the water is deep, and great care when the temperature falls, because it often remains icy under the trees when other places might have thawed, which is why summer is the best time for this ride. It's a very special place, though. Mossy boulders litter the floor beneath tall pine trees, while behind them tower cliffs of Craig y Forwyn and Craig y Cythraul.

World's End isn't the end of this ride, or even the end of the climb: there are another 1.5 kilometres of uphill to go before the final whoosh downhill to Minera. As you press on north you catch a glimpse of the famous Horseshoe Pass 5 kilometres away

on your left, then at the top of the climb you can see Llandegla Forest north-west and a bit above you. There's an incredible mountain bike centre with runs to test all abilities among the trees of Llandegla.

The road undulates towards the top of Esclusham Mountain, where it's pretty exposed. No tree shelter or steep valley sides exist here, but after 2 kilometres of being battered if there's any wind at all, the road descends and the view of the valley Minera lies in opens before you. The descent is quite steep, so take care and brake in good time for the sharp left onto the B5426 that takes you back into Minera.

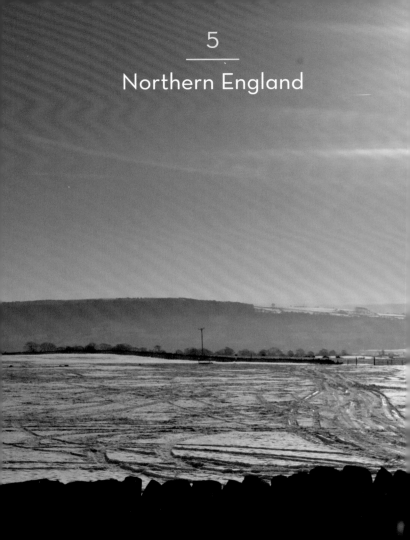

5

Northern England

18 TRANS-PENNINE TRAIL CENTRAL
The hilly crux of a cross-country ride done in a day

WILDNESS RATING **7/10** HARDNESS RATING **8/10**

The Trans-Pennine Trail is a fantastic coast-to-coast route of 215 miles (346 kilometres), stretching from Hornsea on the Yorkshire coast to the Irish Sea resort of Southport in Lancashire. It's fully signposted with Trans-Pennine Trail signs, which have either blue or brown backgrounds, and standard wooden signposts. You can buy maps from the trail's official website, www.transpenninetrail.org.uk, and from a variety of other sources.

The trail covers a wide variety of terrain, from seaside towns to busy ports, through cities and along canal towpaths; some sections follow old railway lines, and a few follow very quiet roads. There are flat sections, undulating ones, and a range of big hills in the middle. Riding the whole thing is an incredible experience.

A few intrepid and very fit souls have done the whole distance in one go, but the Trans-Pennine Trail lends itself to stages, either on consecutive days, which is still challenging, or fitted in whenever you can.

The crux of the Trans-Pennine Trail is crossing the Pennines, the upland area that runs down the centre of northern England, and is a traditional playground for northern cyclists. The challenge of this ride, therefore, is to cross the Pennines using the Trans-Pennine Trail, east to west or west to east, in one go. Retracing your outward pedal to return to where you started doubles the challenge, as well as the feeling of achievement from doing it.

For this description I've taken the eastward journey from Hadfield, which is in Derbyshire and just east of Greater Manchester, to Worsborough

FACT FILE

Where Lancashire and Yorkshire	**OS reference** SE 354 037
Start Hadfield	**Ride distance** 39 kilometres (24½ miles)
OS reference SK 023 959	**Highest point** Gallows Moss (just east of
Finish Worsbrough	Dunford Bridge), 430 metres (1,410 feet)

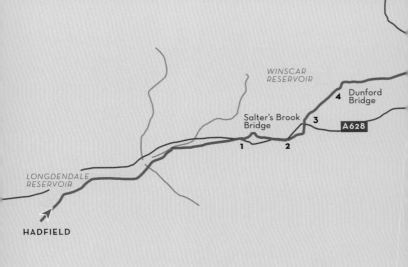

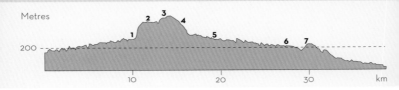

Metres

200 - - - - -

10   20   30   km

TRANS-PENNINE TRAIL CENTRAL
Track Elevation

1   Steep climb then take care crossing the A628. Steep rough track on other side

2   Second crossing of A628, followed by a third

3   Road to Dunford Bridge where you go right after a long descent onto the old rail line

4   Turn left at Winscar Reservoir car park for alternative way across dam wall

5   Long section following old rail line

6   Turn sharp left off old rail line, go right onto B-road then left to four lane end

7   Turn left onto bridleway, then right at rail bridge. This track takes you to Worsbrough

in South Yorkshire, just south of Barnsley. It crosses the entire upland block of the Pennines.

Hadfield is a great place to start, because the car park on Station Road is right next to the trail. Plus it's only 100 metres from the railway station, which has regular services from Manchester. Starting in Hadfield has the added benefit of cutting out the complicated back-streets part of the Trans-Pennine Trail around Manchester and then through and out of Stockport. Hadfield is right on the edge of open country, so heading east there's only wild moorland and a few nice villages ahead of you.

You are soon out of town and into the valley of Longdendale, looking down at the first of a series of six reservoirs in the valley bottom. Longdendale epitomises the central Pennines: it's a deep, dark valley with frowning crags in its upper reaches and, but for high summer when the valley glows with bright purple heather, valley sides that are subtle variations of dark green, ochre and brown.

Continue past the reservoirs, then ride for about a kilometre more, keeping to the right of the River Etherow. The trail then crosses the river and climbs up to the busy A628 Woodhead Pass road. You have to cross

this main road, so take extra care. The trail continues opposite, through a rickety wooden gate and up a rough and really steep track. It's best to walk up it until you are back on more level ground.

Turn right when you come to an obvious trail, continuing along a level section of moorland called Long Side to a second crossing of the A628. Again, take care crossing this busy road. Access to the next bit of trail is almost opposite, through another wooden gate. Once through the gate, descend steeply to Salter's Brook Bridge, before following the trail back to the A628 for a final crossing of this busy road.

The next section of the Trans-Pennine Trail follows a minor road, steeply uphill at first, followed by a long and in places very bumpy descent. In the valley bottom you are in a place called Dunford Bridge, at the mouth of the once famous but now unused Woodhead Tunnel. The Trans-Pennine Trail uses the railway line that ran up to and then through it for the next section of this ride.

But before that there is the interesting option of riding across the massive dam wall of Winscar Reservoir. This offers wonderful views over the reservoir and open moors, as well as down into the valley. Look for the direction sign pointing left about halfway down the bumpy road descent to Dunford Bridge. Turn left, then ride over the dam, then go right after climbing from a car park. Then right again to descend to Dunford Bridge.

Whichever way you choose to reach Dunford Bridge, you need to head east next along the valley bottom, where the Trans-Pennine Trail follows the old railway line. This bit is a joy: it's mostly flat and follows the flow of the River Don, which has its source in the hills just west of Winscar Reservoir. You go through the town of Penistone and into neighbouring Oxspring.

The Trans-Pennine Trail splits in Oxspring: the section that follows the old railway line carries on down the Don Valley towards Sheffield, while the main bit that goes to Hull and the Yorkshire coast involves taking a sharp left off the trail just before a footbridge that takes pedestrians over the trail. Then, shortly after turning left, you reach a road, where you'll see a blue Trans-Pennine Trail sign indicating the bridleway opposite.

You can go that way, but it involves riding a short section of the A629, which can be busy. To avoid that, turn right, ride along a B-road that goes through Oxspring, then take the first left into Four Lane End. Cross the A629, taking care, and follow the road opposite for about 100 metres before turning left on a bridleway that picks up the route of the Trans-Pennine Trail.

The trail splits again just before a railway bridge. Fork right and continue to Worsbrough, a pretty village on the southern edge of Barnsley. This is the end of Trans-Pennine Central, unless you plan to turn around and ride back across the Pennines to Hadfield.

19 THE MARY TOWNELEY LOOP
A challenging and beautiful ride in the central Pennines and a classic wild-cycling loop

WILDNESS RATING **8/10** HARDNESS RATING **6/10**

The Mary Towneley loop circles the upper Calder Valley in Yorkshire and Lancashire, allowing cyclists and horse riders to explore the gaunt beauty of the central Pennines, which is surrounded by the old mill towns of both counties. It's an accessible ride, but the whole loop is testing, so completing it in one go is a wild-cycling challenge.

Mary Towneley was Lady Mary Towneley, a horse rider rather than a cyclist. In 1986 she rode an epic Pennine Bridleway of her own from Hexham in Northumberland to Ashbourne in Derbyshire, in an effort to show how badly the bridleways she used were maintained back then. Her family seat is Towneley Hall near Burnley, so the Countryside Agency, the body that created the Pennine Bridleway, named this 47-mile loop

that includes a section of the Pennine Bridleway and passes close to Towneley Hall after her.

Natural England, the Countryside Agency's successor, also maintains the Loop, which uses bridleways, byways and short stretches of road; the organisation also supplies and erects its acorn signs to give directions. There is an easy-to-use detailed map on the National Trails website, www. nationaltrail.co.uk. Here's the link to it: https://www.nationaltrail.co.uk/sites/default/files/pb_mary_towneley_loop_map.pdf.

The terrain you find on the Loop is mixed. There are cobblestone tracks, some with standard-sized cobbles, others with oversized stones that are more like slabs. There's gravel, grass, some boggy sections and several bits of tarmac, although always little used

FACT FILE

Where The central Pennines of Lancashire and Yorkshire

Start and finish Just west of Hebden Bridge

OS reference SD 977 267

Ride distance 75.2 kilometres (47 miles)

Highest point Top of Leach, 465 metres (1,525 feet)

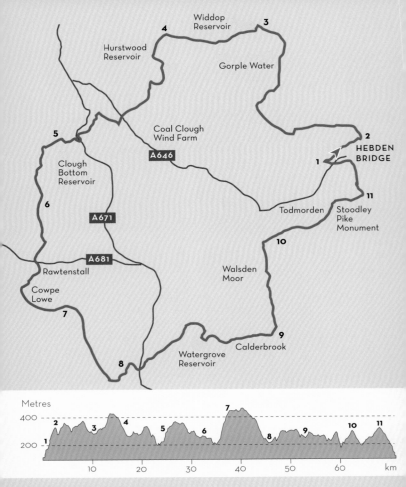

Widdop
Reservoir

Hurstwood
Reservoir

Gorple Water

Coal Clough
Wind Farm

A646

HEBDEN
BRIDGE

Clough
Bottom
Reservoir

A671

Todmorden

Stoodley
Pike
Monument

A681

Walsden
Moor

Rawtenstall

Cowpe
Lowe

Calderbrook

Watergrove
Reservoir

Metres

400

200

10   20   30   40   50   60   km

THE MARY TOWNELEY LOOP
Track Elevation

MAP KEY

1 Start
2 Follow Pennine Bridleway
3 Go left over Widdop Reservoir dam wall
4 Turn off Pennine Bridleway and head south
5 Trail goes south under a double set of power lines
6 Going south from Lumb the ride uses sections of road and trail
7 Follow trail over Cowpe Moss trending east, then go south-east over Rooley Moor
8 The trail loops around the north of Rochdale, crosses a main road, then goes north-east over open moorland
9 Trail hugs valley side going north then crosses the A6035 at Bottomley
10 Trail switches to road then back to bridleway
11 Steep descent back to start

tarmac. The landscape is stunning, but above all it is northern: a muscular mix of old industrial towns, most of which are undergoing rejuvenation, and open moorland. A few woods and glades are thrown in the mix too.

Because it's a loop you can start anywhere and ride clockwise or anti-clockwise, although there is a feeling among experienced mountain bikers – and the Mary Towneley Loop is definitely mountain or cyclo-cross bike terrain – that anti-clockwise is best. I started just west of Hebden Bridge and went anti-clockwise.

The Loop crosses the River Calder just west of Hebden. If you ride out from the town you pick up the trail just after some traffic lights at a place called Charlestown. Look for a trail on your right going up to some houses on the hillside. Careful: the way up to your first reference point on the map, Blackshaw Head, is steep.

This is the section of the Mary Towneley that the Pennine Bridleway follows. Continue north past Gorple Water, then north-west to Widdop Reservoir, then west, crossing from Yorkshire into Lancashire, to where the Pennine Bridleway parts company with the Mary Towneley Loop. The Pennine Bridleway goes north, and the Mary Towneley goes south past Hurstwood Reservoir.

Burnley is on your right now as you cross Worsthorne Moor. This is real Towneley family country now, with Towneley Hall being quite close to Worsthorne. The moors around here were one of Lady Mary's favourite places to ride. Direction-finding is extra easy on this section: you just head south for the white towers and whirling blades of the giant Coal Clough wind farm.

Once level with the wind farm the trail descends to Holme Chapel, and once through the village it runs north-west close to a railway line, then switches south-west to pass along the edge of a small but deep valley. You cross the A671 on Deerplay Moor and, after a trek south-west above Clough Bottom Reservoir, the trail heads south under a double set of power lines.

From wild moor tops you now descend through an increasingly

built-up area before arriving in the town of Rawtenstall in the Rossendale Valley. It's typical of the Lancashire mill towns around here. Once thriving, now being rejuvenated, Rawtenstall grew on the back of the cotton industry, when Manchester became the centre of British cotton-spinning and cloth production.

Lancashire is perfect for spinning and weaving cotton because it gets more rain than Yorkshire. At the same time as cotton was king in Lancashire, however, wool was at the heart of Yorkshire's massive weaving industry. Cotton is delicate: humid conditions make handling it easier. At first it was largely imported through Liverpool, then, after the Ship Canal was built, straight into the heart of Manchester.

With its Ship Canal Manchester became Cottonopolis: a nineteenth-century nickname for the city where a beautiful cotton exchange was built: the place where the cotton barons who owned the mills in Rawtenstall and towns like it made their money, banked their profits and got their lines of credit.

But while vast sums of money were made by mill owners, cotton merchants and bankers, mill workers lived in conditions so poor they inspired a German, Friedrich Engels, working in a mill owned by his father in Salford, to write *The Communist Manifesto* with Karl Marx. (The slaves on the cotton plantations overseas

endured a still worse ordeal, of course.) Marx and Engels's ambition was to create a more inclusive economic and political system that would benefit the many, not the few.

Once out of Rawtenstall the trail climbs up the side of the Rossendale Valley to the left of a flat-topped round hill called Cowpe Lowe. The trail then swings left to cross a craggy open moor called Cowpe Moss, before heading south-east towards Rochdale. It loops around the north of the town where the Co-operative Movement was created in 1844, then heads north-east across wild open moorland again.

There's another change of direction just north of Watergrove Reservoir, east this time, towards Calderbrook, a village on the steep slopes of a valley in which the Rochdale Canal lies. The next section is scenic, but beware of the steep drop of the valley sides on your right as you continue north. You leave Lancashire and return to Yorkshire after 2 kilometres of this stretch, taking a very steep descent to Bottomley, then a very steep climb up the other side of the valley away from the A6033.

The trail then goes around the edge of Walsden Moor, and changes direction to go east on entering Calderdale, above the town of Todmorden. You then pass through Lumbutts and Mankinholes, not a firm of accountants but two attractive hamlets high up in Calderdale, and behold the sight of Stoodley Pike, a

You then pass through Lumbutts and Mankinholes, not a firm of accountants but two attractive hamlets high up in Calderdale…

400-metre-high hill with a needle monument on top.

The 37-metre-tall Stoodley Pike Monument is a landmark seen for miles around Calderdale. It was completed in 1815 to celebrate the defeat of Napoleon at the Battle of Waterloo. The original was struck by lightning in 1854, and the monument seen today was built in its place, with the sensible addition of a lightning conductor. From Stoodley Pike it's only

a couple of kilometres to Hebden Bridge and the end of the Mary Towneley Loop.

It's a fascinating ride, as well as a challenging one if done in a day. The Mary Towneley Loop is of particular interest if you like to know about social history, and it's a ride that rewards studying the route before you ride it – especially reading about the mill towns you go through. One final word of caution: as you would expect, given her history, the Mary Towneley Loop is well used by horse riders, so be on the look-out for them and slow down and take extra care when you pass. Some horses are fine, others easily spooked by cyclists, and you can never tell until they react.

20 THE PENNINE BRIDLEWAY
A long-distance trail ride from Derbyshire to Cumbria

WILDNESS RATING **7/10** HARDNESS RATING **7/10**

The Pennine Bridleway is a managed trail that runs along the spine of England. It's a national treasure, a joy to ride, and in places a cycling challenge worthy of the strongest legs and lungs. The scenery is a mix of stark uplands, green dales and hilly urban fringes, and because of its ease of use the Pennine Bridleway encourages exploration of offshoot routes.

The route is maintained by a dedicated team funded by Natural England and local and National Park authorities responsible for the areas it passes through. It uses bridleways, often old packhorse routes, and minor roads, and caters for cyclists, horse riders and walkers.

Completing the whole trail is a wild-cycling challenge. The Pennine Bridleway is 174 miles long, although there are two extra loops on it that boost the distance to 205 miles. The time you take to complete the ride depends on whether you treat it as a challenge for your body, or an experience for your senses. You can do it all in one go, or ride sections of it over time.

Accommodation is never far away on the Pennine Bridleway because, although most of it feels quite remote, it is never really far from human habitation. The website www.nationaltrail.co.uk/pennine-bridleway is full of information, including an interactive map with accommodation and camping sites marked for those doing a self-supported ride. The website is a must for anyone who wants to ride this trail: you can use it

FACT FILE

Where Along the Pennines from the Derbyshire Dales to the Howgill Fells in Cumbria

Start Just west of Winster on the High Peak Trail

OS reference SK 276 552

Finish Kirkby Stephen in Cumbria

OS reference NY 774 085

Ride distance 278 kilometres (174 miles)

Highest point Shoulder of Wild Boar Fell, 560 metres (1,837 feet)

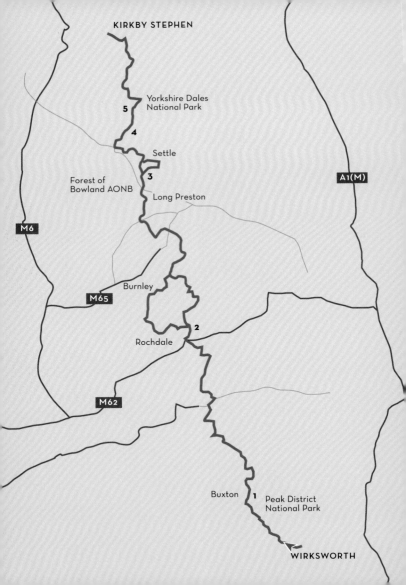

KIRKBY STEPHEN

Yorkshire Dales
National Park

5

4

Settle

Forest of
Bowland AONB

3

Long Preston

A1(M)

M6

Burnley

M65

2

Rochdale

M62

Buxton **1** Peak District
National Park

WIRKSWORTH

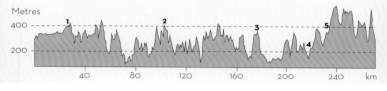

THE PENNINE
BRIDLEWAY
Track Elevation

1 Steep descent into Chee
   Dale, take care
2 Trail splits here. You can
   follow the west or east
   section of the Mary
   Towneley Loop. The eastern
   section of the Loop
   is shorter

3 Start of Settle Loop
4 Trow Gill
5 Cam High Road

to plan your journey, buy maps from it
and even download the entire route
for a GPS device.

People ride the Pennine Bridleway
from either end, but our description
starts in the south, near Wirksworth
in Derbyshire. The trail heads west at
first, using a section of the Midshires
Way where it follows the High Peak
Trail, then it swings north. Direction-
finding is generally quite easy, because
it's marked by National Trails signs
bearing an acorn symbol. You will also
see acorn signs with a colour-code
qualification indicating side trails:
the blue-coloured ones permit access
to cyclists.

Once past the Parsley Hay junction,
where the Tideswell Trail goes south,
keep riding north-west, then north to
Blackwell and the first serious hill
climb. You descend steeply into
beautiful Chee Dale, which is on the

Monsal Trail, another cyclist-friendly
trail that runs along the bottom of a
steep-sided, heavily wooded valley. The
Pennine Bridleway goes straight across
the bottom of Chee Dale, then you
climb steeply up the other side of the
valley. The first scenery change of the
Pennine Bridleway comes shortly after
this, at a village called Peak Forest.

This is the transition between the
White and the Dark Peak, or High Peak
as it's sometimes called. The change is
stark. The rolling green grass, white
scars and deep gorges of limestone
country are replaced by high blocks
of millstone grit separated by deep
valleys, many with reservoirs in the
bottom. There's more climbing now,
as the Pennine Bridleway combines
minor roads and trails to pass through
the western edge of the Dark Peak, and
along the eastern edge of Greater
Manchester.

This is not the most scenic part of the ride, or all that far off the beaten track, but it's interesting. The proximity of high hills and open moorland to the former mill towns of Manchester shows why it was people from here who were behind the Mass Trespass of 1932. This is the name given to the day when a group of social activists marched up Kinder Scout, the highest point in the Peak District, to pursue the right for everyone to roam in open country.

Trespass was illegal back then, even when the land being trespassed on wasn't farmland but open country. Most open country was owned by landlords, and they protected it by forbidding access. A number of the group was arrested and prosecuted, but their action started a revolution that led to a right for everybody to roam in the countryside, albeit on permitted footpaths, bridleways and other trails.

Just past Littleborough, at a place called Summit, you arrive at the first of the two optional loops on the Pennine Bridleway, the Mary Towneley Loop, which is Ride 19 in *Really Wild Cycling*, so you can refer to that ride for the next section as well. Basically, the Pennine Bridleway follows the shorter, eastern section of the Mary Towneley, going around Todmorden as it crosses the Calder Valley. You head north again, where the two halves of the loop join on the moors above Burnley.

Bits of the Brontë Way and Pendle Way take you north, then the Pennine Bridleway heads west towards Barnoldswick and another change of scenery as it enters the Yorkshire Dales. A series of bridleways and minor roads leads to Long Preston, where you have to cross the busy A65

and head for Green Gate Lane, which goes left off School Lane.

Green Gate Lane heads north-west, climbing out of Long Preston, then becomes Edge Lane and after that a bridleway. The bridleway takes you to the start of the Settle Loop, the second extra loop on the Pennine

Bridleway, and the shortest at 10 miles.

The Pennine Bridleway forks left onto Mitchell Lane, skirts the edges of Settle and heads north. To follow the Settle Loop you fork right onto Lambert Lane and ride around an upland area edged with a series of scars – the local name for vertical cliffs

– where the underlying limestone is exposed. You then join the Pennine Bridleway just north of Settle.

After a brief upland ride you descend to Stainforth, where you head east through the village and past Stainforth Force waterfall. Turn right after the camping site and head north again. The bridleway changes direction at the quarries above Helwith Bridge, and you end up going south through a shallow gorge, which is full of caves, to Feizor. Elaine's Tea Rooms in Feizor is well worth stopping at.

Turn right in Feizor just before Old Hall Farm on Hale Lane, and ride around the southern edge of a lovely wooded limestone outcrop. You skirt Austwick next, turning right onto a minor road at the north-eastern edge of this ancient Dales village. Ride for a kilometre to the start of a trail on your right called Thwaite Lane. Follow this trail almost to Clapham, turning right just before Ingleborough Hall on the edges of Austwick to ride along the side of a deep valley called Clapdale.

Trow Gill lies at the top of Clapdale. It's a deep, narrow limestone gorge that starts where Clapdale bends left as your path on the Pennine Bridleway goes right. Trow Gill is a great example of a collapsed cavern. It was formed by waters that now take an alternative route through the Ingleborough Cave and other systems; the waters hollowed out a cavern here until its roof collapsed to form Trow Gill. You get a nice look into Trow Gill from the Pennine Bridleway before the trail veers right to cross the limestone pavement shelf on the east side of Ingleborough.

Areas like this are common in the Yorkshire Dales. They were created by the scraping action of glaciers, and when the ice retreated it left flat areas of exposed rock. Where rain water sits for any length of time on flat limestone, in cracks or other depressions, it tends to dissolve the limestone, because rain water is a weak acid. As the cracks get deeper water lies in them longer, so dissolves more limestone, and creates an effect whereby the limestone looks like it has been cut into blocks. The blocks look like paving slabs from above, hence the term 'limestone pavement'.

You cross the Three Peaks Cyclo-cross route (Ride 22) about three-quarters of the way along this section. Look to your left and you get a taste of the first long slog in that race: it's the toughest one, too, that climbs up the side of Simon Fell. This relatively flat, if a bit bumpy, section ends with a short descent to the bottom of Ribblesdale. You cross the River Ribble, then there's a climb up to a minor road that leads to High Birkwith.

Turn left on the road, and when you get to High Birkwith you continue straight as the road changes to bridleway. This crosses Coppy Gill, a lovely little stream that emerges from Birkwith Cave about 500 metres to

your right and descends over a series of waterfalls to join the River Ribble. Once over Coppy Gill you cross an area of potholes around the valley formed by Ling Gill Beck, then continue climbing up to Cam End on Cam Fell and go right.

The track you follow now, called Cam High Road, traces a much older Roman road. Continue to the point where the surfaced section of the road starts, and look for the Pennine Bridleway sign indicating you go hard left. You descend now to the B6255. Cross the B-road and go west on a surfaced minor road to Newby Head Gate, where you go right.

This bridleway section leads to the top of Dent Fell. Once there you'll see a bridleway on your left descending to Dentdale, but to continue on the Pennine Bridleway stay with the trail you are on and follow it west then north then around Great Knoutberry Hill, then descend to Garsdale Station. Keep following the bridleway past the Moorcock Inn and climb another steep fell-side, continuing left at the top of the steep section.

You cross several streams, most of which are tributaries of the River Ure, on a relatively flat section. Continue to the B2659, where you turn left and follow the B-road south for about 4 kilometres. The Pennine Bridleway continues on your left now, past Hazel Gill to cross the northern shoulder of Wild Boar Fell. Descend to Stennerskeugh, and just beyond the village you go right on the A683 to Kirkby Stephen and the end of the Pennine Bridleway.

21 WOLDS WAY BY BIKE
Shadowing a long-distance footpath on a bike-permitted route

WILDNESS RATING **7/10** HARDNESS RATING **7/10**

Access to open countryside is easier on foot because there are far more permissible footpaths than there are bridleways and other cycling trails. One consequence of such accessibility is the creation of some incredible long-distance footpaths. However, they aren't totally out of bounds to cyclists, at least in spirit. With a bit of map study and careful planning it's possible to shadow many of these great footpaths – indeed, follow their course as closely as possible, and in places share the trails they use.

The Pennine Bridleway does it to a certain extent by shadowing the Pennine Way footpath, although it is nowhere near as long as the footpath. Other cycle trails have done the same, but you don't need to wait for others to create these routes: you can shadow

some great long-distance walks by planning your own route. That's what I did with this ride, the Wolds Way by Bike.

The Wolds Way footpath runs from Filey in North Yorkshire to the Humber Bridge near Kingston-upon-Hull in East Yorkshire. It is 126 kilometres (79 miles) long, and crosses a chalk upland area called the Yorkshire Wolds, which is special. The Yorkshire Wolds have inspired artists and writers, but they are the lesser-known outdoor destination in Yorkshire, which is a shame. If you haven't visited this light-soaked place of rolling hills, open views and hidden valleys, you are missing a treat.

The Wolds Way walk is a great way to appreciate the place, but cyclists don't need to miss out: Wolds Way by Bike shadows the Wolds Way footpath across the Yorkshire Wolds. I went

FACT FILE

Where East Yorkshire	**OS reference** SE 987 252
Start Rillington	**Ride distance** 80.5 kilometres (50¼ miles)
OS reference SE 851 745	**Highest point** Head of Fairy Dale, 194 metres (636 feet)
Finish North Ferriby	

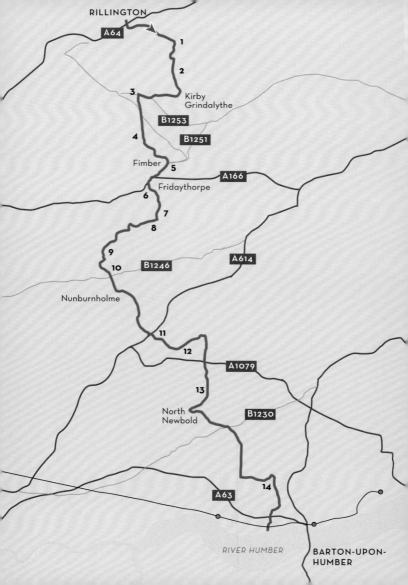

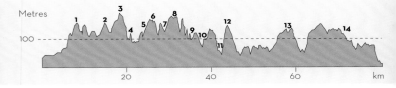

WOLDS WAY BY BIKE
Track Elevation

1 Winteringham Hill
2 Cross a minor road
3 Go left onto bridleway
4 Fairy Dale
5 Go right on B1251
6 Go south out of
   Fridaythorpe on Wolds Way
7 Walk the short footpath
   section to the road to
   Huggate
8 Follow two left forks in
   road, then join the
   bridleway
9 Turn left in Millington
10 Follow bridleway going
   south-east
11 Go left for short stretch of
   A614, then right on the
   Wolds Way
12 Go left on road in
   Goodmanham, then take
   next right to head south.
   Cross the A1079 with care
13 Go straight on bridleway
   where the road bends right
14 Wauldby Scrogs

north to south, but it's just as good in the other direction.

First off, though, the biggest departure I made from the walk. I started Wolds Way by Bike in Rillington instead of the coastal town of Filey. I did so because although there is a nice footpath along the northern edge of the Wolds, which walkers follow before striking out south across them, apart from a few bits classed as bridleway, cyclists can't use it. If I started in Filey the opening leg would involve either riding along a busy A-road or following a long and complicated detour of minor roads and bridleways north of the Wolds, before turning south. It was much simpler to start at Rillington at the foot of the

northern edge of the Wolds, and head south from there.

From Rillington you ride uphill almost straight away. The A64 crossroads in the village, just south of the church, is a good place to start. Cross the A64, then head south-east, and after passing a cemetery follow the road as it veers left, then go left and follow this section of trail to the next crossroads. Go straight on at the crossroads and uphill to Wintringham. Ride through Wintringham, and at the top of the hill turn right on a bridleway. The entrance is opposite a big farm with lots of metal pigsties in a field.

Follow the bridleway south through Green Plantation, past Rayslack House, across a narrow road, and

continue south to Kirby Grindalythe. This lovely village, with a name straight out of *Harry Potter*, is located in a valley now called the Great Wolds Valley, but the Grindal part of the village name indicates it was once called Cranedale, presumably because cranes, a huge wading bird, congregated here. Cranes were widespread in the UK until the 1600s, when their habitats were slowly lost to agriculture, squeezing them out.

Turn right onto a minor road in Kirby Grindalythe, then go past Duggleby, join the B1253 and follow it west for 1.5 kilometres, looking on your left for a bridleway that heads south. Turn left onto the bridleway and ride through Wharram-le-Street,

continuing south to delightful Fairy Dale. This is typical of the secluded dry valleys that are a big feature of the Yorkshire Wolds. They were formed mostly by the action of ice during the Ice Ages, not by water. The chalk they are formed from is porous: so water doesn't flow over their surface, so can't erode it in the same way water does non-porous rock.

There are loads of dry valleys in this part of the Wolds, and they are where farmers keep their stock, growing crops on the hill tops, which is the other way around to how farming works in most upland areas. Yet another reason for the uncommon-looking landscape of the Yorkshire Wolds.

Head for Fimber, where you go right on the B1251 to Fridaythorpe, a village that has hosted the Flat Cap-Throwing World Championships. You've already shared bridleway and road stretches of the Wolds Way; now the route is shared again as you head south on the bridleway out of Fridaythorpe marked 'Wolds Way'. The bridleway runs along the bottom of a narrow dry valley for a while, then on reaching the track to Northfield House you turn right. However, this next short section of the Wolds Way is footpath. It's only 600 metres long, after which the track becomes road, but you must walk the 600 metres.

Once the road starts you saddle up and follow it south to Huggate.

Continue south past the lovely spire of St Mary's Church, which can be seen for miles around, to the crossroads and turn right. Follow this road until it forks, take the left fork, then left where the road forks again, and almost immediately there's a bridleway going off to your right. Follow the bridleway along the top of a dry valley for 2 kilometres, then go right where the bridleway forks. A few metres further on there is a minor road that runs along the bottom of the valley: go left on this road and follow it to Millington.

Turn left at the first crossroads in Millington, ride around the southern edge of the village and take the first left. Ride uphill and follow this road to Warrendale Farm, where you pick up a

bridleway that goes south-east. The
bridleway is level at first, crosses the
B1246 and runs through Wold Farm,
then downhill through Bratt Wood to
Nunburnholme. Follow the main road
through the village and turn right to
go uphill. The hill is one of many
throughout the UK that has been used
by cyclists for a particular form of
torture called a hill climb. Hill climbs
are races: competitors start at
one-minute intervals and are timed
from the bottom to the top of a hill; the
fastest time wins. Be warned: they hurt!

Once at the top of Nunburnholme
Hill continue on the road south to
Londesborough. Turn right at the
T-junction, then first left to the
roundabout on the A614. Go left for a
short stretch north-east on the A614,
just for half a kilometre, looking on
your right for a bridleway. There's a
picnic spot there called Towthorpe
Corner. Turn right onto the bridleway
and you are back sharing the Wolds
Way with walkers, so keep a look-out
for them. Follow the Wolds Way
through Goodmanham, but go left on
the road that the Wolds Way crosses
before continuing on a footpath.

Follow the road, which after
2 kilometres bends right at 90 degrees.
You are going south now. Continue
across the A1079, taking extra care
crossing, then south to where the road
bends right at 90 degrees for a second
time. Go straight on at that bend,
following a bridleway south. This

becomes a road, then meets another
on Newbald Wold. Turn right onto that
road and ride to North Newbald.
Take the first left as you enter North
Newbald, then after 200 metres go left
again and follow this lane over the
B1230. Go right at the next junction,
then straight at the one after, heading
for Riplingham.

Continue south through
Riplingham, then go left at the next
crossroads to follow a bridleway, riding
across open country first, then along

the northern edge of a wood called Wauldby Scrogs, a name worthy of a character in Dickens. Towards the eastern end of Wauldby Scrogs the bridleway turns south: follow it through and out of the trees, then south-east to where it meets a little lane. Go right on the lane, then left, and continue through Swanland to join the B1231.

Follow the B1231 over the A63 to North Ferriby, once home to William Wilberforce, the independent MP for Yorkshire from 1784 to 1812 and leader of the movement to abolish the slave trade. Keep heading south through North Ferriby, and after a kilometre you reach the north bank of the massive River Humber. This is the end of the Wolds Way by Bike. The Humber Bridge is just east of here – you can't miss its huge towers and 2.22-kilometre span. The Wolds Way meets the Trans-Pennine Trail on the north bank of the Humber, so a whole host of bike challenges opens up here.

22 THE THREE PEAKS CYCLO-CROSS
A long distance cyclo-cross race in Yorkshire

WILDNESS RATING **8/10** HARDNESS RATING **9/10**

This is a race, and you can only do this route by competing in it, because special permission from landowners and other bodies is required for cyclists to ride it. The Three Peaks Cyclo-cross is a tough challenge but well worth doing, even if it's impossible to ride all the way. Some sections see even the fittest competitors running with their bikes, and carrying them up brutally steep slopes. Just finishing the Three Peaks is a badge of honour: you need a track record in off-road challenges just for your entry to be accepted.

The Three Peaks are Ingleborough (703 metres), Whernside (736 metres) and Pen-y-Ghent (694 metres). They are all in the Yorkshire Dales National Park, and linking their summits in a 40-kilometre (25-mile)(ish) loop has been a walker's challenge since two teachers from Giggleswick School did it in 1887.

They went round in ten hours, and slowly the walk gained notoriety and momentum. By the 1930s many fit young walkers were doing it inside five hours, and the first official Three Peaks running race was held in 1954, the Cumbrian fell runner Fred Bagley winning in 3 hours, 48 minutes.

Then in 1959 a fourteen-year-old Skipton schoolboy, Kevin Watson, completed the Three Peaks route on his bike, riding where he could and carrying and pushing his bike where he couldn't. Watson's time was 6 hours, 45 minutes, including a total of 1 hour and 17 minutes when he stopped for rests.

A very good cyclist and experienced road racer, John Rawnsley, read about Watson's ride in

---

FACT FILE

Where The Yorkshire Dales
Start and finish Helwith Bridge
Os reference SD 812 995

Ride distance 60.8 kilometres (38 miles)
Highest point Whernside, 736 metres (2,414 feet)

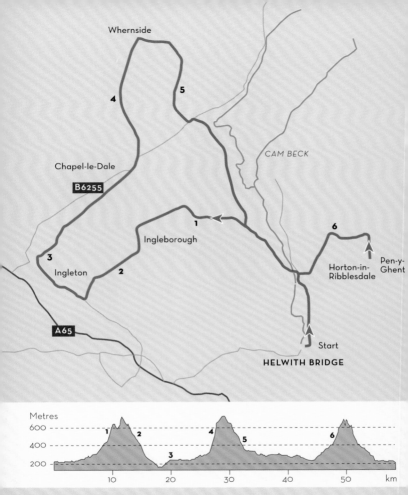

Whernside

5

4

CAM BECK

Chapel-le-Dale

B6255

1

6

Ingleborough

3

Horton-in-
Ribblesdale

Pen-y-
Ghent

Ingleton

2

A65

Start

HELWITH BRIDGE

Metres

600

400

200

1   2   4   5   6

3

10   20   30   40   50   km

THE THREE PEAKS CYCLO-CROSS
Track Elevation

MAP KEY

1 The steepest sections up Ingleborough are impossible to ride, you have to carry your bike up them

2 Ingleborough's descent is technically demanding

3 Long road section

4 The steepest parts of Whernside are ultra-demanding

5 The descent from Whernside is technically demanding, especially the slab sections

6 The ascent and descent of Pen-y-Ghent is the least difficult of the three, but it is still very tough

a Skipton newspaper and was inspired. He got some of his Bradford Road Cycling Club mates together to have a go at the Three Peaks route.

'It was a sort of hard riding-club run the first time,' Rawnsley told me in 2012. 'We tried it one Sunday in 1960. We started in Ribblehead; there was me, Harry Bond, Geoff Whittam, Ron Bows and Pete O'Neil, and we climbed Whernside first, then Ingleborough, then Pen-y-Ghent. I made a record of all the intermediate times, the punctures and the falls, and our final time was 4 hours, 31 minutes and 31 seconds.

'We did it again in May 1961 and lowered the time to 3 hours, 54 minutes. So I decided to organise the first Three Peaks Cyclo-cross race on 1 October 1961. There were thirty-five starters, including a world championship cyclo-cross rider, Bill Radford from the Midlands. We went the same way as the fell race does: Pen-y-Ghent first, then Whernside and finally Ingleborough, starting and finishing at Horton-in-Ribblesdale. I won, from Harry Bond.'

In all Rawnsley organised the Three Peaks Cyclo-cross fifty times, and raced forty-five of them, only stepping down from organising in 2012 at the age of seventy-five. He took up running after the first Three Peaks Cyclo-cross, so he could take part in the Three Peaks running race. He completed that thirty times, and walked the Three Peaks too. At the last count he'd crossed all the Three Peaks in one go, either by bike, running or walking, well in excess of 150 times.

The Three Peaks has been won by some of Britain's best cyclo-cross riders. Some Europeans have had a go, too, but only the Swiss rider Arthur Mainz ever won (1981). The Three Peaks Cyclo-cross is a special race, one in which running meets cycling. Many winners have fell-running experience, and the current victory record-holder, Rob Jebb, with eleven wins, is one of the best fell and mountain runners in the world.

Running is such a big factor in the Three Peaks Cyclo-cross that you should include some running, as well

as lots of carrying your bike up steep slopes, in your preparation. The route has always had significant sections that are impossible to ride. Other sections can only be ridden with excellent off-road skills. Training for the Three Peaks should include as much off-road cycling as you can do, some running, some bike carrying, and practising skills like bunny-hopping your bike.

The Three Peaks Cyclo-cross route has changed since its inception. With give and take between the organisers, landowners and other interested parties, the route is longer now: 61 kilometres, with more road sections. The order of peaks has changed too: it goes Ingleborough, Whernside, then Pen-y-Ghent now.

Training for the Three Peaks should include as much off-road cycling as you can do, some running, some bike carrying, and practising skills like bunny-hopping your bike.

You start and finish in Helwith Bridge. The first section is on the road and neutralised, because the competitors must ride behind the race organisation's lead car, which doesn't dawdle. Neutralisation ends after Horton-in-Ribblesdale, with a sharp left turn onto the first off-road section, Gill Garth.

You are now climbing towards the summit of Ingleborough, gently at first, but it quickly gets steep, then very

steep. This is the first long uphill bike carry. There's some respite crossing Simon Fell, but the final slog to the summit is brutal. It's so steep you sometimes have to use a free hand to grab tussocks of grass to help haul yourself upwards.

After being checked by marshals past the summit cairn there's a long bumpy descent to Cold Cotes, then a road section through Ingleton and Chapel-le-Dale to Bruntscar, where the climb of Whernside begins.

Not quite as tough as Ingleborough, but still requiring a long bike carry in the first third, Whernside is mostly rideable after that. Once over the top there's a long descent across Blea Moor to Ribblehead. Like all three descents it requires total concentration.

Past Ribblehead Viaduct there's a long road section down to Horton-in-Ribblesdale, where the climb of the third peak, Pen-y-Ghent, begins. You go left up a rutted lane between dry-stone walls. The track is rideable at first, but take care because it's the same way up and down, so you'll meet other competitors coming in the opposite direction.

The last bit of Pen-y-Ghent is steepest, then all that's left is the last bone-juddering descent and a short road section back to Helwith Bridge and the finish. The winner usually gets round in three hours. Those inside 3 hours, 30 minutes are deemed elite; inside four hours is first class; inside five is second, and all other finishers get a merit certificate.

23 SALTER FELL BOTH WAYS
Follow the Romans across some of the finest moorland scenery in the north of England

WILDNESS RATING 8/10   HARDNESS RATING 8/10

This ride is in the beautiful Lancashire district of Bowland, a place for connoisseurs of wild cycling and hill walking. At its heart is Salter Fell Track, a bike-accessible off-road trail that follows the course of a Roman road.

Salter Fell Track was described by no less a figure than Alfred Wainwright, author of the beautiful seven-volume *Pictorial Guide to the Lakeland Fells* and many other wonderful titles, as 'the finest moorland walk in Britain'. Wainwright is one of the most influential contributors to the body of English wild literature, so his recommendation is to be taken seriously.

The ride is simple. It starts in Hornby close to where the River Wenning flows into the Lune, and goes south-east across the uplands of Bowland to Slaidburn in the Hodder Valley. It's a tough ride, so it's a good idea to refuel at one of several good cafés in Slaidburn before retracing your outward journey back to Hornby.

Salter Fell Both Ways is best done in summer, or in dry spring and autumn conditions. The track across Salter Fell is rideable, mostly, but it's stony and gets muddy in places if it has rained a lot. The ride requires good bike-handling skills, plenty of fitness and lots of patience. This is not one to rush: the views are incredible – open, free and really wild. The upland areas are largely covered by heather, bog and some wild pasture, while the valleys support a wide variety of trees, many them descended from a much larger Forest of Bowland than the one that remains today.

Hornby is dominated by its castle, a much-extended country house built on the site of a smaller medieval castle

FACT FILE

Where Northern Lancashire	**Ride distance** 47 kilometres (29½ miles)
Start and finish Hornby	**Highest point** Salter Fell Top, 419 metres (1,374 feet)
OS reference SD 584 686	

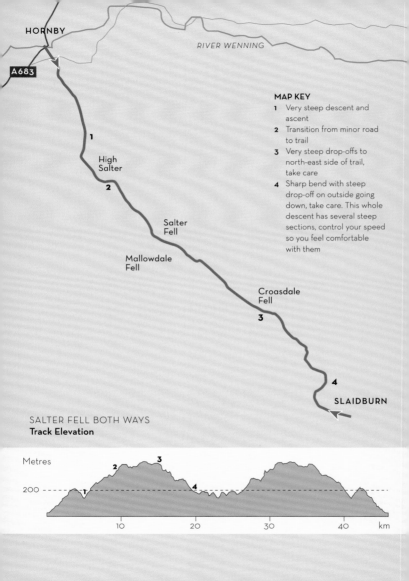

HORNBY

RIVER WENNING

A683

MAP KEY

1 Very steep descent and ascent

2 Transition from minor road to trail

3 Very steep drop-offs to north-east side of trail, take care

4 Sharp bend with steep drop-off on outside going down, take care. This whole descent has several steep sections, control your speed so you feel comfortable with them

High Salter

Salter Fell

Mallowdale Fell

Croasdale Fell

SLAIDBURN

SALTER FELL BOTH WAYS
Track Elevation

Metres

200

10   20   30   40   km

from the thirteenth century. The church near the centre of Hornby is a good place to start. Ride south on the A683, then cross the River Wenning and go straight on where the main road bends sharp right. If you look back over your left shoulder at this point you get a great view of the castle. Don't look too long, though: the climbing is about to begin, and there is rather a lot of it.

The first kick up is steep, then the gradient doesn't really relent that much for the next 3 kilometres up to a place called Thornbush. You are still on a surfaced road at this point, albeit a narrow and infrequently travelled one. Through Thornbush you descend steeply to cross the River Roeburn, which flows off Salter Fell. It has formed a very steep-sided valley, and all along it tributaries rush and tumble down, some over waterfalls, swelling to Roeburn on its journey north.

The road kicks up steeply again after crossing a bridge over the Roeburn, and through Lower and Middle Salter. Then, after 2 kilometres of tough uphill, you arrive at Upper Salter. Take a breather here to look across the Roeburn Valley to the opposite fell, Mallowdale – it's magnificent. The off-road section, Salter Fell Track, begins now.

It's still uphill for a good way yet. Less steep at first, but the gradient racks up at Higher Salter Close, so the final 1.5 kilometres to the Salter Fell summit, and the highest point in the whole ride, is very steep. There is some reward, though: the summit section is a joy. The trail undulates gently for 4.5 kilometres, crossing a plateau first, but that leads to a shelf for Salter Fell Track to run along the side of White Hill. The terrain slopes away quite sharply on your right and rises at a similar angle on your left.

The shelf section is about 2 kilometres long, then the terrain either side of the track opens and you start to descend. Take care going down, though: the track descends in steps and the drops are quite steep. You are following the valley of Croasdale Brook, although much higher up its side. The first steep drop comes after you go around a shoulder of land on your right: the track bends sharp right,

then goes steeply down. The best thing to do here, and in general riding off-road, is to reduce speed when you can't see the track in front of you.

There's a flatter section across Low Fell, then another right bend and a steep drop to where the track gives way to surfaced road. Follow this road, which is nothing more than a narrow country lane, to a T-junction. Turn left at the T-junction and descend to Slaidburn.

This village, now in Lancashire but once part of the West Riding of Yorkshire, will be very familiar to brass band enthusiasts. 'Slaidburn' is a quick march, composed by William Rimmer, that is a standard in the repertoire of brass and silver bands.

Have a leisurely break in Slaidburn if you've time. It's a lovely old village, built where Croasdale Brook flows into the Rider Hodder. The view north up the Hodder Valley towards the fells behind Stocks Reservoir is perfect. Anyway, you need to give yourself time to digest if you eat there, because the return journey starts by climbing back up the hill you descended.

Take the first right once out of Slaidburn, then there are two more kilometres of surfaced road before you are back on Salter Fell Track. It's just a question of retracing your outward ride back to Hornby now, and the Salter Fell Track is really worth doing twice. It looks a lot different going back – most cycle routes do – but if you really don't

want to ride the same route again there are some great return routes using the little lanes to the north and south of the Salter Fell Track.

The roads are really quiet, and the surrounding terrain is pretty wild too. You'll need an OS map to find the way. The northern return goes north-west from Slaidburn up the Hodder Valley. There's only one road to follow for

most of the way, then you go left to Wray, which is 3 kilometres south-east of Hornby. The southern route goes via Dunsop Bridge, then you take the famous Trough of Bowland road to Caton for a short stretch of the A683 north-west to Hornby.

This is a great route, and riding off-road across an upland area exceeding that magical 400-metre contour is always a challenge. It's the views, though, that sell this one, plus the feeling of being in the wild without being remote. If you are lucky you might see a hen harrier, a bird of prey making a tentative comeback here, and orchids grow wild beneath the trees in the valleys. The whole of Bowland is a delight, and Salter Fell Track is a perfect way to experience it.

24 COAST-TO-COAST, PART ONE:
ST BEES TO KIRKBY STEPHEN

The first half of an incredible ride across the roof of
northern England from the Irish Sea to the North Sea

WILDNESS RATING **9/10** HARDNESS RATING **9/10**

There are many coast-to-coast cycle routes, but this is the classic, the hardest and arguably the wildest. It's also the closest to Alfred Wainwright's walkers' route, and like Wainwright's the Coast-to-Coast cyclists' route passes through three National Parks: the Lake District, the Yorkshire Dales and the North York Moors. The ride is committing, the scenery incredible and varied. This high-level ride across northern England is both a joy and an achievement to do.

It starts and ends in the two places Wainwright chose to start and end his classic walk: St Bees in Cumbria and Robin Hood's Bay in North Yorkshire, and it passes through many of the same places. The muscular mountains of Cumbria and remote northern Dales are separated by a short stretch in the Eden Valley, then you get a longer respite across the undulating Vale of Mowbray, before clambering up the Cleveland Hills and over the North York Moors to an abrupt end at one of the jewels of the North Sea coast.

The vast majority who do the Coast-to-Coast ride it in stages, either during a holiday or tackling sections as and when they can. Many holiday companies offer guided or supported rides, with guests staying in various levels of accommodation, of which there is plenty along the route. Others do the Coast-to-Coast by bike-packing, camping at various points and carrying all they need with them. But whichever way you choose, spending

FACT FILE

Where Cumbria	**OS reference** NZ 953 049
Start St Bees	**Ride distance** 126 kilometres (78¾ miles)
OS reference NX 971 117	**Highest point** Black Sail Pass, 537 metres (1,761 feet)
Finish Kirkby Stephen	

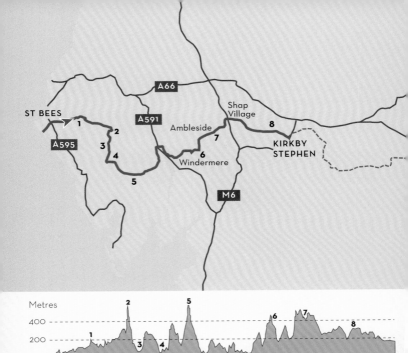

COAST-TO-COAST,
PART ONE
Track Elevation

1 Ennerdale Water
2 Black Sail Pass. Hard
   work going up, technically
   demanding descent.
   Both sides require section
   on foot
3 Wast Water

4 Eskdale
5 Walna Scar Road
6 Kentmere
7 Shap Fell
8 Gentler back lane ride
   to Kirkby Stephen

nights under a roof or under canvas, this ride requires planning and research, especially if you are doing all the planning yourself.

A detailed description of this route, as well as the detailed maps or other forms of navigation, are beyond the scope of this book. The Coast-to-Coast requires a book of its own, and luckily there are plenty to choose from. Lots of good guidebooks and websites are dedicated to the Coast-to-Coast ride. You'll also need the correct maps and/or downloads for a GPS device. And it's worth reading Wainwright's own *A Coast to Coast Walk* guide to provide some background, as well as revel in his words and beautiful hand-drawn illustrations.

Finally, what type of bike is best for riding the Coast-to-Coast? Well, although there are quite a few sections of road in the Coast-to-Coast, some of the off-road sections, especially in the Lake District, are very rocky and technical. This ride is definitely more suited to a mountain bike, especially during the Lake District section.

Given the above, the job I've set myself by including the Coast-to-Coast in *Really Wild Cycling* is to provide a feel for it, hopefully persuade you to try it and draw attention to what's in store if you do. I've split the ride into two, so here goes with part one of the Coast-to-Coast.

St Bees stands on the Irish Sea coast of Cumbria. It's an ancient place that has grown from the foundation of a seventh-century convent dedicated to St Bega. It's a quiet place looking out over the sea, framed by the red cliffs of St Bees Head to the north and some of the highest mountains in Great Britain to the east. They are where you are going first.

The Coast-to-Coast uses some minor roads and an old railway line to cross part of what was the industrial western fringe of the former county of Cumberland. Back in 1974 local government reorganisation rolled up Cumberland and Westmorland, stuck parts of Lancashire and Yorkshire in with them, and called the whole thing Cumbria.

After 13 kilometres you reach Ennerdale Bridge, and the first of many scene changes on the Coast-to-Coast. The village straddles the lovely River Ehen, which flows out of the Lake District's westernmost lake, Ennerdale Water. This is where the Lake District starts.

Continue east on the track that runs along the north shore of Ennerdale Water, and an incredible

The Coast-to-Coast uses some minor roads and an old railway line to cross part of what was the industrial western fringe of the former county of Cumberland.

view is revealed the further east you go. Standing behind the lake, from left to right, are the peaks of Bowness Knott, Starling Dodd, Red Pike, High Stile, Angler's Crag and Crag Fell. Then further up the valley the majestic Pillar comes into view. It's breathtaking, and there's lots more to come.

The terrain hasn't been too demanding so far, but that changes with a vengeance at Black Sail Hut, where you turn right to climb the viciously steep slopes of Black Sail Pass, gaining 250 metres of height in just 2.4 kilometres. The surface is rough and rocky: most of the Lake District is of volcanic origin, and volcanic rock is tough. It's probably better to walk most of this climb,

pushing your bike. It saves energy and it's easier to stop, turn around and take a few moments to admire some of the best mountain scenery in Britain.

The view over Ennerdale north towards Haystacks is incredible. And it's well worth mentioning Haystacks because Alfred Wainwright, who is with you in spirit throughout this ride, had his ashes spread on top of that beautiful mountain, close to Innominate Tarn. The view north from the summit of Haystacks, down the Buttermere valley, was one of his favourites. There are also incredible views from the summit of Black Sail. Pillar and Kirk Fell tower above you, each of over 800 metres, while looking

south you see Mosedale, where the descent from Black Sail leads.

This is a steep downhill, so take care and walk the bits you aren't confident of riding. Black Sail Pass is probably the steepest and gnarliest part of the whole Coast-to-Coast ride, so take heart because progress won't always be this slow. Mosedale leads to Wasdale Head at the top of Wastwater, the deepest lake in the UK in the remotest valley in the Lake District. Wasdale is home to the legendary Joss Naylor MBE, fell runner supreme, whose feats of human endurance are mind-boggling. He's eighty-three now but still runs, works and walks in this lovely, lonely valley.

Moving south, the next pass you cross is lower and easier than Black Sail, but no less spectacular because at the top you are flanked by Scafell and, above that, the highest mountain in England, Scafell Pike (977 metres or 3,205 feet). This pass leads to Eskdale, from where you climb over the southern shoulder of the Old Man of Coniston on a bridleway called Walna Scar Road, a favourite with local mountain bikers. Walna Scar runs for 10 kilometres; some bits are well surfaced, but a lot of it is rocky and demanding. It's another place to take extra care and ride well within your skills.

A minor road section leads to Skelwith Bridge, then it's off-road to Grasmere and along a lovely track by Rydal Water to Ambleside. From there a road section leads to Waterhead and an off-road crossing to Troutbeck and Kentmere, with two good bits of high ground in between.

The scenery changes after Kentmere. You follow an old road north that climbs up a craggy gorge of the type most commonly associated with the Lake District, but then swing east and emerge into the more open and smoother scenery of the Shap Fells. It can be wild, wet and windy up here, and Shap village has a frontier feel with its single street that straddles the A6. Shap Summit lies just to the south, and is a major difficulty for cyclists riding the Land's End to John o' Groats, especially for anyone attempting to set a new record for this massive ride. Shap also gave its name to a granite quarried here, which you will have seen even if you have never visited Shap. The granite is pink when polished, often flecked with other colours, and is seen in a many great buildings all over the UK.

Shap is also the gateway to the final section of the Coast-to-Coast Part One. A mostly back-lanes ride leads to Kirkby Stephen, a small town with lots of cafés and accommodation, so an ideal staging post on this ride. With 126 kilometres of hard country already covered, though, you will have probably had an overnight stop by now. You are still in Cumbria, just: the Yorkshire border is 4 kilometres away, and that's where the Coast-to-Coast goes next.

25 COAST-TO-COAST, PART TWO: KIRKBY STEPHEN TO ROBIN HOOD'S BAY
The Yorkshire half of this epic ride across northern England

WILDNESS RATING 8/10 HARDNESS RATING 8/10

This is the longer of the two sections I've broken the Coast-to-Coast ride into, but it's slightly less severe than the first. It's still challenging: it crosses two upland areas divided by the flat Vale of Mowbray and ends at the coast, so it has four distinct sub-sections. That means four changes of scenery, each special in its own way.

The section starts with 2.5 kilometres of the main A685 going north out of Kirkby Stephen, but most of the rest of the ride is off-road or uses very minor roads. It also crosses some really wild country. You leave the main road at Winton and begin climbing around Winton and Kaber Fells to cross into Yorkshire just before Tan Hill, famous as the location of the highest

pub in England, the Tan Hill Inn. Tan Hill lies on the Pennine Way walker's route, so it's a major crossroads for cyclists, walkers and runners who love places like this. It's high and wild, you are well above the 500-metre contour and there are very few trees, so little shelter, but on a clear day you can see for miles and the air is full of natural rather than man-made sound.

Continuing south, you cross Stonesdale Moor on the way to Keld, a tiny cluster of stone houses and farms near the head of dramatic Swaledale. The rapid River Swale rushes through the village, tumbling over a series of low waterfalls as it does so. Keld is also the start of the first trail section of the Coast-to-Coast Part Two, which follows the Swale as it

FACT FILE

Where From Cumbria across North Yorkshire	**OS reference** NZ 953 049
Start Kirkby Stephen	**Ride distance** 155 kilometres (97 miles)
OS reference NY 775 091	**Highest point** Tan Hill, 527 metres (1,729 feet)
Finish Robin Hood's Bay	

rushes through Gunnerside to Reeth.

Alfred Wainwright called this way the 'Royal road to Reeth'. He also observed that high Swaledale is Norse country: the place names Keld and Thwaite have Norse origins, as do the names people gave to geographical features here, like gill, fell and foss. Lower down Swaledale the names are more Anglo-Saxon in origin.

Swaledale was a stronghold of the Brigantes, a Celtic people who lived here before the Roman invasion and occupied a country called Brigantia, which was almost as big as and had a similar footprint to Yorkshire today. The Brigantes resisted Roman occupation of their lands with great force. They inflicted damage on the Roman armies and slowed up their strategy for England. Some think that Hadrian's Wall was built to prevent the Brigantes combining with the tribes of Scotland, which would have been a handful for the Romans. In any case, it took them a long time to bring Brigantia under Roman rule, and just being in Swaledale makes you see how this wild country bred such feisty warriors.

This road and trail section ends at Grinton. You cross the Swale to Fremington, then after Marrick you are back riding off-road almost to Marske, a gorgeous village set amid limestone cliffs. A lovely bridleway runs alongside the cliffs up the valley of Marske Beck, but that's for another time. Pressing on north-east you climb halfway up a steep hill, then a trail section takes you past more limestone cliffs and into Richmond.

It's worth spending time in Richmond, because the town is steeped in history, from its castle with a massive Norman keep, to its marketplace surrounded by ancient buildings and watched over by Holy Trinity Church. Richmond is also where you start across the gentle undulations of the Vale of Mowbray.

Follow the B6271 east from Richmond, then south from Scorton, and when you are level with Ellerton you turn into a minor lane and follow it east to Wiske, then Brompton, then Ellerbeck. This bit is all on the road and includes a section of the main A684, but the roads are mostly quiet. Consider it a zone of transition across the pastoral scenery of the Vale of Mowbray while anticipating the huge bulk of the North York Moors, which grows ever bigger as you go on.

The climbing starts straight after you ride under the A19. The eastern and northern edges of the North York Moors are steep, and at this point they are called the Cleveland Hills. You climb a steep minor road up through Osmotherley, to where a trail spears off right into some woods at Scarth Nick. A network of bridleways and old mine roads leads the Coast-to-Coast to Raisdale and a tiny village called Chop Gate. Different minerals have been mined on the North York Moors for

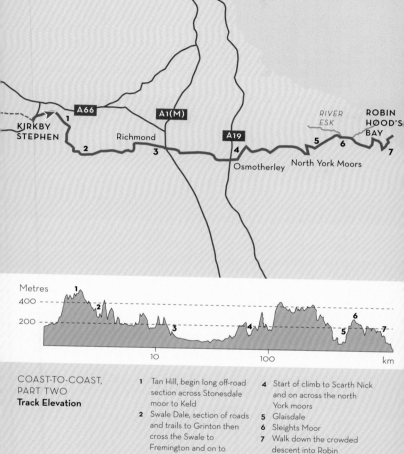

A66
A1(M)
A19

RIVER ESK

ROBIN HOOD'S BAY

KIRKBY STEPHEN

1

2

Richmond

3

4

Osmotherley

North York Moors

5

6

7

Metres
400
200

1

2

3

4

5

6

7

10   100   km

COAST-TO-COAST,
PART TWO
Track Elevation

1 Tan Hill, begin long off-road section across Stonesdale moor to Keld

2 Swale Dale, section of roads and trails to Grinton then cross the Swale to Fremington and on to Richmond

3 Start of flat section across northern edge of the Vale of Mowbray

4 Start of climb to Scarth Nick and on across the north York moors

5 Glaisdale

6 Sleights Moor

7 Walk down the crowded descent into Robin Hood's Bay

centuries; most of the mining has gone now but the roads and railway lines created to serve it now provide hundreds of miles of useable trails for cyclists.

The route continues east along a bridleway that leads to the summit of Round Hill, where ancient cairns, the work of Norse or Anglo-Saxon people, show this upland area was widely inhabited in their times. From here you also get a great view of Middlesbrough, which owes its growth to the minerals mined in these hills.

Getting onto the North York Moors involves some serious climbing, but now the route ingeniously slips around the heads of several valleys that dissect this high plateau. It's a great section to ride: you can see for miles over the different valleys. Farndale and

Rosedale are particularly attractive. This part is quite easy riding, too, but that comes to an end as you descend from Glaisdale Rigg into Glaisdale. There's more climbing to come, and it keeps coming right to the very end.

Glaisdale Beck flows into the River Esk, which the route follows east to Grosmont, a quiet village now, but Grosmont once had an ironworks whose furnaces lit the night sky and could be seen from miles around. You go south from the railway station in Grosmont, which is used by the steam trains of the North York Moors Railway as well as Northern's Esk Valley Line. Two footbridges take you across an Esk tributary called the Murk Esk, then you follow the trail uphill to a minor road and continue climbing to the top of Sleights Moor.

More trail leads through a forest and into and out of a narrow valley. From there the route is quite complicated. You follow a minor road north past a spectacular waterfall called Falling Foss, which is really worth seeing. To do so, you ride a bit further north, then take the first left, which has a signpost to May Beck car park, and follow that lane down. The car park is next to the waterfall.

Whether waterfalls are your thing or not, the next section crosses Fylingdales Moor, the easternmost of the North York Moors. The final phase of the Coast-to-Coast starts with a descent towards Boggle Hole and its famous youth hostel; then there's the sting in the tail, a tough road climb to Fyling Hall.

There are only 2 kilometres from the top, and they are downhill. The view over the tilted rooftops of Robin Hood's Bay and out over the North Sea is breathtaking. Enjoy it, but be careful on your bike: the descent to the beach is steep, and in summer there are often so many pedestrians on this road it's safer and less stressful to all concerned to walk down .

Robin Hood's Bay is a picturesque holiday destination now, but its secluded place in the bay it's named after originally helped it grow as a centre for smuggling. Back then smuggling was a well-run, big and highly lucrative business here.

In the 1800s lots of big ships chose Robin Hood's Bay as the place to offload their cargoes. They did it by anchoring in the bay while small boats

were rowed out to meet them. The small boats took the cargoes ashore in multiple batches, where the goods got transferred to carts to be checked by excise men, or pussyfooters as the locals called them, and have any duty applied. At least, that's what should have happened.

The thing was, there were so many ships, and even more little boats and carts going to and fro, but never enough customs men – the locals and the ships' captains saw to that. A lot of high-excise items, like tobacco and alcohol, miraculously disappeared off the carts into houses and were passed from one another by means of secret doors all the way up the hill, to emerge later at the top of the village. From there the contraband was mixed with more innocent stuff on carts or packhorses and transported across the moors for onward distribution.

Robin Hood's Bay is of course the end of the Coast-to-Coast. If you dipped your wheels in the Irish Sea at St Bees you might want to dip them in the North Sea here – it is a Coast-to-Coast tradition. This is an incredible ride, probably one of the best in Britain, because it is so varied, so interesting. It's tough, but it's rewarding. In his book, *A Coast to Coast Walk*, Alfred Wainwright ended with these words: 'I finished the Pennine Way with relief, the Coast-to-Coast Walk with regret. That's the difference.'

26 BACK O' SKIDDA'
A mountain circuit in the quiet northern Lake District

WILDNESS RATING 7/10 HARDNESS RATING 8/10

The Lake District offers plenty of wild-cycling experiences, but most are well populated by all kinds of outdoor enthusiasts. This ride offers something wild but different. It's away from the tourist traps, the busy places – away even from the main off-road cycling routes. It is set in the stark but beautiful mountains of a less frequented part of the Lakes known locally as Back o' Skidda', meaning 'the other side of Skiddaw'. Skiddaw is the northernmost of the Lake District's four 3,000-foot mountains, and Back o' Skidda' refers to the hills behind, or to the north of it.

The Back o' Skidda' ride is a mix of tiny lanes, off-road trails and abandoned mine roads, and winds over two long climbs and descents, the first across the Caldbeck Fells and the second up and over the pass between Skiddaw and the Uldale Fells. There's an undulating section in between. It's about 40% narrow lanes and 60% trail. A mountain bike is probably best for this one, but a skilful and strong rider could do it on a cyclo-cross bike fitted with very robust tyres.

Mosedale is probably the best place to start. It's a tiny village, but it's the biggest on this ride, and starting from here you get a flat first kilometre to get your body moving. Ride north out of the village, staying on the main lane and ignoring any side trails. After the first flat kilometre the road starts rising; get used to it.

Head for Calebreck by taking the left fork at the next junction. Just before you reach Calebreck look for an abandoned mine road on your left: it starts just after a cattle-grid sign, and there's an information board at the road entrance. Once on the mine road and heading generally west, you need

FACT FILE

Where Northern Cumbria	**Ride distance** 33 kilometres (20½ miles)
Start and finish Mosedale	**Highest point** Little Calva, south side,
OS reference NY 357 321	490 metres (1,607 feet)

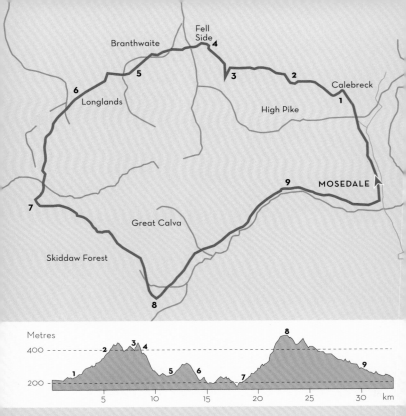

BACK O' SKIDDA'
Track Elevation

1. Turn left and follow abandoned mine road west
2. Keep right at trail junctions
3. Area of difficult navigation, follow the faint trail south then north-west in a V shape
4. Turn left and follow narrow lane to Howburn
5. Trail section from Howburn to Longlands
6. Join road at Longlands and continue south-west to Peter House Farm
7. Go left on trail to cross valley north of Skiddaw to Skiddaw House
8. At Skiddaw House go left and follow the trail to the road in the Caldew Valley
9. Go east on the road and ride to Mosedale

to keep right where you see any other trails joining it. Eventually you pass two disused mines; the second is next to High Pike, a conical fell directly south of you at this point and another 250 metres higher.

Carry on riding west, then, just before the terrain dips sharply down into the steep-sided valley of Dale Beck, look for a quite faint trail on your left. Go left and follow this south, going uphill for 300 metres. You then reach a small shelf of flat land, and you'll see another quite faint trail that almost doubles back on the one you have just followed, and heads north. Turn very sharp right, almost 180 degrees, and ride north, descending now, then swing north-west following the trail to a place called Fell Side. This complicated diversion is easier to follow when you are there on the

ground, and is necessary to avoid some bits of difficult terrain.

Fell Side consists of a few houses and two farms on either side of a narrow lane: it's the lane you're after. Turn left and follow the lane south-west to Howburn, where you pick up a good trail to Longlands. You reach another narrow lane in Longlands: go left on the lane and follow it south-west for 4.5 kilometres before looking left for the gap created by Dash Beck between the Uldale Fells and the giant Skiddaw.

Peter House Farm is your marker: it's behind some pine trees and on your right. Dead opposite, so on your left, is the entrance to the next trail section. There's a wooden signpost on your left, and two metal gates separated by a wooden one. Dismount and use the wooden gate, then mount up and head

south-east. You soon start to climb. Go right at the first fork, then the valley ahead becomes narrower and the trail gradient even steeper.

Continuing south-east, you'll see Dead Craggs on your right, which are impressive and may have been the source of Skiddaw's name. Skiddaw comes from the ancient Norse, in which *skut* is a word that can describe a jutting crag, and *haugr* means hill. There are other explanations for the name, though.

Once you get level with the middle of the crags you reach the start of a really steep section of the trail. Luckily the surface is good, but this bit is a slog, as it takes you up a big step to where Dash Beck flows over Whitewater Dash waterfall.

The gradient relents at the top of the waterfall, which is quite noisy and spectacular when plenty of water flows down Dash Beck. Continue south-east: the trail crosses some flatter, more

marshy ground, but then rises to Skiddaw House, an independent hostel that is the highest in Britain and in a stunning location. It's completely off the grid too; no other houses are in sight, it's 3.5 miles from the nearest road and there is no phone signal. If you want peace and quiet, Skiddaw House is the place for you. Read about it on www.skiddawhouse.co.uk.

Skiddaw House also signals a change of direction, and a nice respite

from all the slogging up hills you've been doing. It's situated at the watershed for this part of the Back o' Skidda' fells. Dash Beck and the River Caldew are born 50 metres apart in the same boggy spring, but Dash Beck flows west and the Caldew flows east. You follow the Caldew from here.

Take a left just before Skiddaw House, and follow the Cumbria Way. It's downhill almost all the way now to Mosedale, but the trail conditions are worse. The way down is bumpy and very cut up in places. There's a sharp left after 500 metres to a small bridge over the Caldew: cross it and the river flows down to your right for the rest of the way, although you cross several tributaries before the bridge over Grains Gill Beck. Shortly after that the rough trail meets a surfaced turning circle used by motor vehicles, and you follow a surfaced road for the final 3 kilometres to Mosedale.

The long descent provides an enjoyable end to this ride, and the valley you are in, called Mosedale, is serene. Only shepherds work here now, but there used to be mining at the head of Mosedale. Carrock wolfram mine was sunk in pursuit of the copper ore, galena, but actually yielded an ore of tungsten commonly called wolfram, but more correctly wolframite. Back o' Skidda' is not a long ride, but quite a tough one, and a joyful wild-cycling experience.

27 FROM SEA TO SOURCE
Following a river from its mouth to its source

WILDNESS RATING **7/10** HARDNESS RATING **8/10**

Following a river from the sea to its source is a fascinating challenge. It can even be an adventure. The Victorians went on perilous journeys to discover the sources of the worlds' great rivers, and following a British river by bike is a physical and geographical challenge I couldn't pass up for this book. It doesn't have to be a huge river: many UK rivers measure 10 or so miles from mouth to source, but the exercise of following their course involves a good understanding of maps, of how rivers work, and an instinct for seeking out a good route.

I chose a jewel of the north-east for this ride, a river that helps tell the story of the countryside it runs through: the River Wear. It rises among the high fells of the northern Pennines, and flows through the home of County Durham's ancient leaders, the Prince Bishops, through the glorious city of Durham to meet the North Sea in Sunderland. It's a tough ride – 120 kilometres (75 miles) from start to finish, and inevitably uphill most of the way – but a beautiful one that combines minor roads, converted railway lines and plenty of bridleways.

From Sea to Source starts on the north side of the River Wear at Roker, a much-rejuvenated seaside town with a lovely sandy beach. It also has a great bike café, Fausto Coffee, right on the seafront, perfect for last-minute carbohydrate loading. The first section goes through a built-up area and it's complicated, but it follows Sustrans Route 7, so it's well worth buying the Sustrans *County Durham & North Yorkshire Cycle Map* from their online shop, www.sustrans.org.uk. It's well

---

FACT FILE

Where North-east England	**OS reference** NY 800 433
Start Roker	**Ride distance** 120 kilometres (75 miles)
OS reference NZ 408 588	**Highest points** Top of Weardale, 627 metres (2,057 feet)
Finish Top of Weardale	

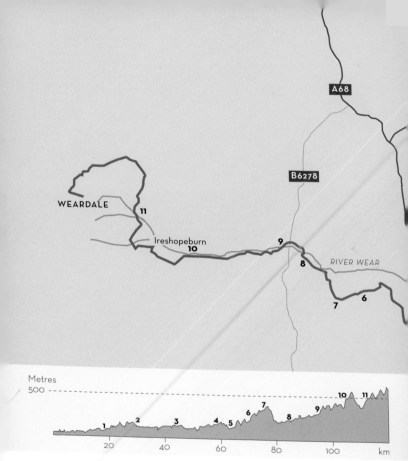

WEARDALE

Ireshopeburn

RIVER WEAR

A68

B6278

Metres
500

20   40   60   80   100   km

FROM SEA TO SOURCE
Track Elevation

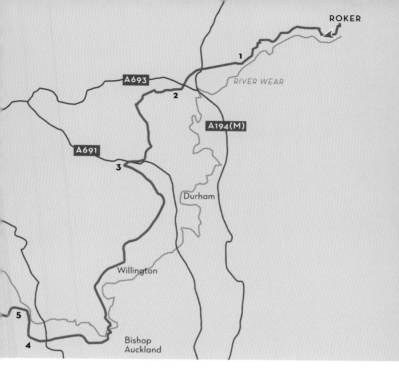

MAP KEY

1 At North Hylton the route leaves the banks of the Wear and follows Sustrans route 7 at the rail bridge after south Pelaw

2 Follow the B6313 west then go first left to Edmondsley then Sacriston

3 Join the cycle route at Langley Park and follow it east then south-east past and on to Bishop Auckland

4 Turn right at crossroads and follow this road through woodside, then cross the A68. Go right at next crossroads, then right again and pick up the bridleway next to the Wear

5 Follow this bridleway to the next road and continue west, high up the valley

6 High moorland section along mine road

7 Go right off mine road and descend towards A689. Turn left before crossing the bridge

8 Cross the Wear and ride through Stanhope

9 Cross the Wear again level with last houses of Stanhope then follow the wear west to Daddry Shield

10 Follow mine road on left just before St John's Chapel. Turn right and walk along footpath to road down into Ireshopeburn

11 Go right on B6295, the left after Allenheads. Turn left onto A689 and ride east to a car park at the source of the Wear

signposted, but the map gives a bit of route-finding reassurance.

You follow the north bank of the Wear for the first 7 kilometres, which was once home to Sunderland's shipbuilding yards and is still known by the name it was then, Wearside. Shipbuilding made Sunderland famous throughout the world, and it gave rise to the nickname people from the city became known by: Mackems. The name comes from the phrase in the local dialect, 'Mack 'em and tack 'em', which refers to the shipbuilders making the ships and local pilots taking them down the river for their customers to take over.

At North Hylton the route deviates north from the river to get around some marshy ground; then you ride through a waterfowl park and are reunited with the river until the 12.5-kilometre mark. At this point Sustrans Route 7 picks up an old railway line and heads west, away from the river, and you follow it. There are a few compromises like this, where there isn't a cycle trail or even a road next to the river, but you are never that far away and, apart from a couple of necessary deviations, the route follows the Wear valley, which is called Weardale, although sometimes quite high up the valley side. This is part of the challenge of following a river to its source with a nod to staying wild: planning a cycle-accessible route that follows the river as closely as possible but at the same time following less-travelled ways.

Continue on Sustrans Route 7. You go under the A693, past South Pelaw to Pelton Fell, where the trail goes under a road bridge and you leave Sustrans Route 7. Just before the road bridge there's a footpath running alongside the trail to your right. Dismount and carry your bike over to the footpath and follow it, walking, for the few metres up to the road, where you go left and over the bridge, so over Route 7. Turn right at the next T-junction, left at the one after, and left again at the one after that. Go right on the B6313, then first left to Edmondsley and then Sacriston, birthplace of former footballer and England team manager Sir Bobby Robson.

At the crossroads in the centre of Sacriston you go right and follow the B6312 to the roundabout with the A691. Take the second exit following the A691 for 800 metres to the next roundabout, where you take the first exit to Langley Park. After a kilometre, and just after the bridge over the River Browney, look for a car park. Enter the car park and there's another cycle trail using the route of an old railway line. Join the cycle trail and head south-east.

This is a really enjoyable section of From Sea to Source, as direction-finding is easy: just follow what is a fairly level trail to Bishop Auckland, while cycling though open countryside and some interesting places, old and

new. There is also a fantastic view of Durham with its castle and cathedral, a UNESCO World Heritage Site perched high on a spectacular cliff overlooking a huge U-shaped bend in the River Wear.

Durham city can be traced back to AD 995. Its university is the third oldest in the country after Oxford and Cambridge, and the city is big enough to be impressive but small enough to feel intimate. Durham is really worth visiting if you haven't already, and you can leave the trail and follow Sustrans Route 14 to ride right into the city centre and back to the trail.

In years gone by Durham was so far from London that its bishops ruled Durham County, levying their own taxes, appointing officials and even making and enforcing their own laws. Such was their rule and control that they became known as the Prince Bishops. Apart from one, who was an Earl Bishop, every Bishop of Durham from 1071 to 1836 was called a Prince Bishop, even though the later Prince Bishops weren't ruling Durham. Over time they also decamped from the city and moved to the bishop's hunting

You follow the north bank of the Wear for the first 7 kilometres, which was once home to Sunderland's shipbuilding yards and is still known by the name it was then, Wearside.

lodge, which was extended and a town, Bishop Auckland, grew up around it.

Follow the trail past Brancepeth Castle, then through Willington and, as you approach Bishop Auckland at 51 kilometres into the ride, look for a picnic site just before the town: this is your mark to leave the trail. Follow the road from the picnic site under the A689. Turn left at the T-junction and follow this street through the first houses of Bishop Auckland to join the B6282. Follow the B-road south, then west out of town, over a roundabout to a crossroads, where you turn right.

The Wear, having made a big change of direction in Bishop Auckland, is now on your right-hand side and will be most of your way up its valley. Follow the road you are on through Woodside, then across the A68, then go right at the next crossroads and right again at the junction after that. A bridleway starts opposite the next T-junction: follow it alongside the Wear, then along one of its tributaries, Bedburn Beck.

After a while the bridleway swings uphill to a road. Go right on the road to Bedburn, where you cross over Bedburn Beck. Go left at the next two T-junctions, but 100 metres after the second junction look for an old mine road on your right. Turn right onto the mine road, which you follow for 4.25 kilometres across open moorland